I Am Fearless

12 Elements of Fearless Living

By
Debbie Leoni

Great Little Book Publishing Co., Inc.

Great Little Book Publishing Co., Inc.
Sacramento, CA

I Am Fearless — 12 Elements of Fearless Living
by Debbie Leoni

Copyright © 2016 Debbie Leoni

www.greatlittlebook.com

ISBN # 978-1-942115-12-0

Fearless Living is about being a contribution,

being responsible, not only for
yourself, but your
role in the world,

getting out of your own way,

being fearless
for the sake of the whole.

-Debbie Leoni

Contents

Foreword

Learning from the *Fully Expressed* Perspective on Fearlessness

by Jenifer Novak Landers, life coach, speaker and author of the book Fully Expressed Living.

Working, coaching and co-creating with Debbie Leoni for over 7 years is a very exciting part of my career. I am thrilled to share her vision for "Fearless Living" and being part of bringing it into the world.

We work using similar processes, coaching philosophy and approach to our clients, and have enjoyed being each other's coach, business advisor, mastermind partner and co-creator through many triumphs and challenges.

I bring my business perspective of "Fully Expressed" into creating the twelve elements of fearless living by saying, "When the twelve elements are fully expressed, the power of Fearless Living IS unstoppable."

My personal choices to be fearless are what gives me the tools I need to lift myself and others into greater fulfillment. I'm quite sure I have the best coach EVER in Debbie Leoni.

Throughout the creation of this book, we have challenged each other to take fearless actions as if there wasn't any other choice. My life and business have benefited in huge ways. This is why convinced and committed that this book makes a wonderful impact on the world.

One of my favorite quotes is by Marianne Williamson who in us to embrace our fully expressed selves by asking us, "Wh you **NOT** to be brilliant and amazing?"

This quote says beautifully that it's our FEAR keeping us diminished, and small, and that often we fear shining our brightest light. I am willing to face this fear, because I figure if I can choose to be courageous expressing my own brilliance and power, I can handle anything else.

Debbie and I have asked each other in a variety of scenarios, "What if your greatest contribution is simply a full and intentional expression of your gifts into the world?"

I love the opportunity through our coaching conversations to realize that no matter how or where I bring my creativity and passion into form, this is an expression of leadership. When I can master and fully embrace one element in my life, it becomes a form of leadership.

I am grateful for my connection to Debbie. I'm inspired by her tireless work for creating this context of Fearless Living – I am farther ahead on my path as a result.

Yes, the world needs each of us to take the lead in this way.

nward with your fearless self, fully expressed!

h
e.
'm
act

vites
o are

My Fearless Stand

As I reflect on how I was led to supporting others
in living fearlessly, I have such gratitude.

I am grateful for all the adversity in my life,
the events that had me paralyzed in fear,
the let downs, the relationships that ended,
the setbacks, and the stuck feelings
I experienced through it all.

Because of all my life experiences,
I am able to guide, challenge and support others
in shifting the energy from fear to courage.

With gratitude,
I take a stand for fearlessness.

"Debbie Leoni's insights and lessons are transformative to readers who are done playing small and ready to move up into the "major leagues" of professional, personal and financial success. This book is a "how to guide" for those ready to convert fear into courage. Debbie offers tools and processes to move you out of the limitations of fearful thoughts and behaviors and into a mindset of fearlessness where one is capable of achieving their full potential. My life is forever changed by Debbie's work."

Barry Freeman,
Managing Director and
Head of Healthcare Investment Banking,
Lincoln International

Introduction

"Thank your fearless self for allowing you to grow as big and strong as you've ever wanted to be and for giving you the strength to speak your truth and be your authentic self in ways you've never imagined."
—Debbie Ford

Many years I procrastinated about writing a book.

Why? Because I was afraid. Afraid that it wouldn't be good enough, long enough, factual enough, the list of "not enough" goes on and on.

I made up excuses that I really didn't have a story that would make a difference. My stories are insignificant. My book won't make a difference so why bother writing it. So I didn't.

My resistance continued to eat away at me as I was always so envious of my friends and colleagues who became authors. I lived in my fear for years.

The day came when I decided I better start practicing what I preach; FEARLESSNESS! I have always prided myself in being strong and courageous. In fact, my friends, clients and family have always given me that feedback. "You are so strong, Debbie." "I wish I had your courage." Ha! What a joke!

Fast forward to today: I did it and it feels indescribably wonderful. If this book touches your life, then I feel blessed. If it doesn't, know that this was written from a place of courage.

My intention for this book is to help you to use your fear versus your fear using you.

Fear is not a bad thing.

It's there knocking on your door and it won't go away, until you embrace it and use its energy to move you powerfully into the life that you desire.

Fear is here to eliminate your suffering and heal your heart in ways that you never imagined.

When my fear shows up in my awareness, I now use it as a tool; an emotion filled with information that can propel me into something greater.

I love my fear because it's really the same as courage.

It's a choice.

My Personal Story

It took years for me to step through my fear of leading my first live event. I designed a two day event called "Fearless Living". I procrastinated and sabotaged my progress because of my thoughts that kept me playing small.

I was in a swarm of fearful thoughts such as, "I'm not good enough to do this. I'm not capable. I might not make an impact. What if I fail?" The list seemed endless.

Then one day as I had done in the past, and with the help of my coach, I realized how toxic those thoughts were. I realized how I was denying the world of my gifts and passion. I became aware, once again, that if I didn't take this step, I wouldn't be living in integrity with what I value most.

Even though I was fearful, I did it anyway.

That's what it takes. I promoted the workshop, all the while allowing my anxiety to be alongside me and not in the driver's seat. I created a workbook. I marketed, I enrolled and since then hundreds of lives have been touched.

I conquered my fear, moved through it and experienced the rewards!

Next thing I knew, I was faced with another fear! The truth is, fear never goes away and that is a very good thing. Fear continues to call us to our next level of spiritual and emotional evolution!

My events were successful beyond my dreams. Several of the attendees came to me and said: *"I want to know more! I want to learn more! I want to share Fearless Living with other people!"*

The same swarm of fearful thoughts returned: "You can't do that! You are not capable, good enough, experienced enough!" My tired old story reared its beautiful head to show me I had another opportunity! Now this was beyond scary! The thought of designing a training? Me? No way!

I knew my fear was "messaging me", that this was the obvious next step for my business. I was ready to embrace a higher level of integrity, contribution and fearlessness! I was even more afraid this time than I was in launching the Fearless Living Event. Yet I did it anyway!

I designed an intense 9-month program to teach the concepts, tools and strategies that I use with my clients. The result? It became the most powerful experience of my life AND the students felt the same way.

Fear was alongside me throughout and courage was in the front seat! The hero, once again, is fearlessness!

Fearlessness is in each and every one of us! You get to access it to create the life of your dreams and what I believe is even more important - fearlessness will have you be the biggest contribution you can possibly be to the world because you won't let anyone or anything get in the way of living the highest expression of you. You won't let anyone or anything get in the way of using your God given gifts, talents and passion to change the world!

We all have a choice every day: to play small, or to defy gravity, to step into possibilities and soar. That can only happen with fearlessness

Join me in saying every day, "I Am Fearless!"

YES, "I am Fearless!"

"We rise by lifting others." -Robert Ingersol

My work as a life coach began with a passion for helping others grow, heal and transform.

Over the years, I noticed a common theme working with my clients: FEAR. Being afraid was the only culprit holding them back from the life of their dreams!

I saw that the growth and freedom I want to teach is only limited by their fearful thoughts and beliefs.

I designed workshops and coaching programs around the goal of embracing fear in order to have a full and successful life.

The results my clients were getting continued to inspire me to go deeper into supporting a fearless approach to living, and soon the idea of Fearless Living was born.

I am passionate about taking this topic as far and wide as possible through my work. My perspective encompasses all levels of personal growth being possible through the topic of fearlessness. I believe it can lead us directly into the ultimate goal in a life well lived: Abundance on all levels.

Understanding Fearlessness

"Everything you've ever wanted is on the other side of fear." – George Addair

Fearless Living is expressed in multiple versions. We see people living fearlessly all around us. We all express fearlessness in many areas of our lives, some louder or quieter than others, and always with potential to grow.

Fearless Living is an ongoing awareness, an ongoing practice and an ever-unfolding path of growth.

Seventeen Examples of Fearlessness

1. Doing what it takes to create the life you desire.

2. Being honest in every relationship to serve the highest good.

3. Being comfortable with the unknown and the mystery of life.

4. Getting out of your comfort zone and taking risks.

5. Seeing the highest good in every situation.

6. Doing everything to the best of your ability.

7. Letting go of who you think you are for who you can become.

8. Standing in the highest vision of yourself.

9. Opening to possibilities.

10. Considering relationship with self and others as sacred.

11. Letting go of perfection.

12. Taking daily action.

13. Detaching from outcomes you have no control over.

14. Being an inspiration.

15. Setting and maintaining healthy boundaries.

16. Being impeccable with your word.

17. Approaching life as a student, with an open and curious mind.

A Spiritual Perspective

"Fate loves the fearless." –*James Russell Lowell*

It's my belief that in order to live the life that you deserve, to be your best and to make your dreams become real, you must have a relationship with the power that is greater than you.

You may refer to this as Source Energy, the Universe, God, or your Higher Power. No matter what your frame of reference, to be fully expressed, you must live outside of the smallness of the self and exist within the presence of something greater.

Fearless Living is a path in life that calls us into our greatest potential, and the path that most connects us to God. When I consider the ultimate destination of taking this path, it makes sense to me that a spiritual component is inevitable.

To live fearlessly is to stand in a life that is rich in all areas. The destination is abundance. Wealth fully expressed on all levels: Physically, emotionally, mentally and spiritually.

If you ask me how I would describe the foundation and purpose of Fearless Living, it would be about experiencing a personally fulfilling level of abundance in and of everything.

The Twelve Elements of Fearless Living

Twelve single elements make up the big picture of Fearless Living, each element offering an expression of the necessary components of an abundant life.

The twelve elements are a challenge and an invitation to grow, broaden our perspective, break through limitations, embrace our power and express our full potential.

Each element stands on its own as a valuable resource and opportunity.

When all twelve are combined, the result is a powerful journey through the deepest and most meaningful pursuit in life, "following your dreams and achieving the joy of fulfillment."

The highest intention for Fearless Living is every human being enjoying unlimited abundance and fulfillment.

12 Elements for Fearless Living

Personal Leadership, Boundaries Commitment, Choice, Projection, Integrity, Surrender, Forgiveness, Acceptance, Intuition, Presence and Honoring Self.

PERSONAL LEADERSHIP	BOUNDARIES	COMMITMENT
CHOICE	PROJECTION	INTEGRITY
SURRENDER	FORGIVENESS	ACCEPTANCE
INTUITION	PRESENCE	HONORING SELF

When you make a conscious decision to align your life with the twelve elements, you are naturally requesting support of your greatest success and abundance. Through visualizing this, you are actively creating it.

Three Ways to Take a Stand for Fearless Living: Integrity, Communication and Trust

Make a strong statement for your fearlessness by taking a stand in three powerful ways:

1. Integrity: You must take a stand for following through with your commitments.

Integrity is described as "doing what you say you will do" and "walking your talk". Integrity is being willing to live your values no matter what the circumstance.

2. Communication: You must take a stand for communicating clearly, purposefully and openly.

Fearless communication demonstrates respect at all times. Your communication empowers yourself and others when you are complete and intentional. Effectively communicating produces desired results, connection and resolution.

3. Trust: You must take a stand to gain trust through consistent action.

You must take a stand for developing higher levels of trust in yourself and with others. Fearless Living invites you into trusting your intuition. The power of trust shows up in everything you say and do.

Journaling Exercise

Write about how you can change or improve your experience with the three ways to take a stand.

Acknowledge your strengths, and acknowledge what you can learn from the areas where you fall short or need to improve.

(Write a short paragraph for each of the three ways to take a stand.)

Fear is Keeping You Stuck

"I'm fearless, I don't complain. Even when horrible things happen to me I go on." -Sofia Vergara

What gets in the way of living fearlessly?

The majority of participants in my workshops and programs come in with little to no clarity about what ignites their deepest passion.

They also know that something is holding them back, as they are continuously falling short of what they say they want in certain areas of their lives.

Here are three steps to move from stuck to fulfilled:

Step 1: What's my passion and purpose?

In order to live a life fully expressed, it requires that you know what has you feeling passionate and purposeful, because ultimately this is what has us living the life of our dreams. Without this clarity, you might feel like you are wandering aimlessly through your life, never really knowing what it is that has you feeling unsatisfied, frustrated or stuck.

Once you are able to identify what makes you tick, what lights up your internal fire and has you feeling passionate, then you get to take the next step!

Step 2: What's stopping me?

What thought or belief is it that is preventing you from living your passion and purpose? Without understanding what's going on in your internal world, how will you even be your best? And I can guarantee you that what is stopping you from living your vision is nothing outside of you. It's an inside job. Those self-limiting beliefs about yourself, whether conscious or unconscious, are obscuring your vision. Those beliefs are telling you "I can't do it, I'm not capable, I will fail," and on and on and on.

You must identify those fearful stories you tell yourself because they are critical in creating the change you desire. Most people will often push those fears away by distracting themselves with external influences such as: shopping, drug, alcohol, food, sex, technology, etc.

Once you've identified your fear, you then have power over it! Fear is just an energy that, with a new perspective, you can change into courage!

Step 3: What do I need in order to "Do it Anyway"? Ok, so now you know what you are afraid of. AND, you also now know that you have 1 of 2 choices. Allow your fear to continue to drive your behavior towards staying stuck OR do whatever it takes, even when you are afraid.

You get to choose! Nothing will change until you decide and commit to doing it anyway!

Journaling Exercise

Write your PERSONAL answers to these important questions:

- *What's my passion and purpose?*
- *What's stopping me?*
- *What do I need in order to "Do it Anyway"?*

Make sure you come up with one specific action for each question.

Step Out of Your Comfort Zone

"Do the thing you fear most, and the death of fear is most certain." - Mark Twain

Our zone of perceived safety feels comfortable and familiar. We are used to being in this zone, only it delivers a huge "Booby Prize" every time we choose it because we THINK we are comfortable and safe when in reality we are limited and suppressed and unable to access our greatest potential.

What keeps us feeling "safe"? Isn't it ironic, this illusion of "safety/ comfort" amidst all of our fearful thoughts, words and actions?

On a biological level, your fear protects you when you feel danger and it tells you to hide within the limitations of what you think you know.

Yet fear keeps you in a trance, an illusion of safety; one that limits you from experiencing anything other than what's familiar to you. The ego holds on to fear so you can escape reality and believe that it's too dangerous to accept the truth of your situation, your circumstances, and your life.

Instead, what if you made a new commitment to yourself and allow your fear to awaken you to notice what is real? Because when you decide to touch what is real, your heart awakens and calls you back home to your essential self; the parts of you that have been lying dormant. You see, the heart does not lie. The lies or illusions only come from the mind/thoughts/ego.

What if you decided to let the guardian of your comfort zone (fear) take a back seat and rest, so that you can access your heart and step outside the egoist trance and into your awakened self?

Last, say to yourself "May my current situation serve to awaken my heart and mind to wisdom, compassion and healing."

Journaling Exercise

What comfort zone am I living in?

What keeps me from seeing my reality as it is?

If I could eliminate fear, and remove the veil of my comfort zone, what new reality could I experience?

Reflection Exercises

In my years of practice coaching others, leading workshops and training others in my programs, I use a powerful process I call a "Reflection Exercise."

I created these reflection exercises to access a deeper experience of self-awareness.

Reflection exercises are critically important for a deeper level of personal work, and more importantly, they provide lasting transformation and results my client's desire.

The purpose of a reflection exercise is to move away from being "in our head" and move into our heart, or our feeling center.

Reflection exercises are a powerful way to integrate information into experience.

Reflection Exercise:
Become Aware of Your Fears

This reflection exercise develops self-awareness about your fears. Use it toward the result of releasing them.

Find some time to be quiet, alone and contemplative.

Close your eyes and allow yourself to remember the last time you felt passionate and purposeful.

Allow yourself to feel those feelings as if you were reliving that time in your life.

As you become present to those feelings, ask yourself: "If I were to create the life of my dreams and be fearless, what would my life look like?"

Then, ask yourself "What fear is preventing me from living my vision?"

Feel that fear, notice where you feel it in your body.

Then notice how long you have felt that fear and how long it has held you back.

Last, ask yourself "What will I do today to DO IT ANYWAY? What action can I take, even if I'm afraid, to move me powerfully towards feeling passionate and purposeful?"

You have everything you need to shift fear into courage.

Tell yourself daily "I am capable, I have everything I need in this moment where I choose to live fearlessly" and watch miracles happen.

Complete the reflection exercise with a few minutes of journaling about your experience.

Ready for More?

Reflection Exercises, Guided Meditations and additional resources for Fearless Living are available online:

www.debbieleoni.com

The Key to Fearless Living: Accountability and Self-Responsibility

Before we move into the exploration of the Twelve Elements, we need to establish an empowering structure. In order to make the most of the Twelve Elements, we need the support of a strong mindset.

Accountability is a structure that enables your success. Responsibility is the key for getting the most out of your journey ahead.

Being accountable and taking self-responsibility are your two intentions for creating success through all twelve elements of Fearless Living.

Self-Responsibility means taking charge of your thoughts, words and actions. Being accountable to self and to others means holding your thoughts, words and actions in the highest context.

Defining SELF-RESPONSIBILITY:

When you are willing to act independently and make decisions without authorization, you are demonstrating responsibility to yourself and to others around you.

Living fearlessly is about taking the initiative to respond with action in all areas of your life.

SELF-RESPONSIBILITY in Action:

Oftentimes, being responsible requires that we take actions we might not necessarily want to take. Being responsible for ourselves is about taking risks, completing tasks, or showing up in ways that will have you feeling uncomfortable.

Another aspect of self-responsibility is asking for what you need. A true leader does not sit back or shut down when feeling overwhelmed, unclear or unsure. Owning your commitment to fearlessness is a self-responsibility path.

Defining ACCOUNTABILITY:

Accountability is the tool that supports your commitment to being 100% responsible. Accountability is the willingness to account for the choices you have made and are making. It's my experience that accountability has a "bad rap" for many because they interpret it as judgment and feeling wrong.

See accountability to your ticket to learning from your choices, versus making yourself or another wrong or not enough.

ACCOUNTABILITY in Action:

Hold accountability as an obligation to yourself so that you can learn and respond to the choices in your life that are working as well as the choices that are not working.

Powerful Questions

**Asking questions brings awareness and growth.
Use powerful questions as an inquiry into your daily
routine in order to make room for choosing thoughts,
beliefs and actions that feed your flame rather than
diminish your flame.**

What gets in the way of using accountability?

What do you need to stay on track?

What's working in my life?

What's not working in my life?

What can I learn from the choices I made?

PART ONE:
THE 12 ELEMENTS

Be truthful, gentle and fearless. -Gandhi

In this section you will learn:

The fearless perspective of each element, explained through beliefs, qualities and examples of Fearless Living.

BELIEFS – support our ability to succeed. Positive beliefs promote fulfillment. Limiting or fearful beliefs promote negativity and failure. It's up to us to become aware of our beliefs and to choose the belief that aligns with our intentions for living fearlessly.

QUALITIES – represent aspects of ourselves we can choose to express for the greatest good. Understanding a new concept in terms of the qualities it expresses is a powerful way to embrace the concept at a more meaningful level.

EXAMPLES – give us the power of stories to understand how the elements play out for ourselves. In the context of a story about someone else's experience we can find the wisdom and insight we need. Stories about our human nature allow us to celebrate the hero in each of us.

The Spiritual Perspective on Fearless Living

God didn't give us the spirit of fear, but of power, love and self-control. — 2Timothy 1:7

Taking our perspective into a broader context, let's look at the twelve elements from a spiritual perspective.

Let's begin with a definition of Spirituality:

Spirituality is your personal relationship with your higher power. It is your own personal belief system that expresses who you are in the world, in all areas of your life, all the time.

Your relationship with your higher power is one, just as in all relationships, that needs to be nurtured daily.

The twelve elements have a spiritual aspect because they influence the unfolding of spirit from the invisible world of our soul or our inner world, into the visible world of action and expression.

Viewing the elements from a spiritual perspective is about taking them to heart and applying them the same way we would apply a principle such as telling the truth to someone, or being fair with someone.

This context of spirituality gives us a way to embrace each of the twelve elements in a deeper way.

Definitions of God

One way to add a spiritual perspective on Fearless Living is to consider the definition of God. There are endless ways to define God, and in alignment with our definition of spirituality, it is a PERSONAL relationship.

I will share definitions of God given by several top spiritual thinkers alive today, including Deepak Chopra, Carolyn Myss, Marianne Williamson, Wayne Dyer, Michael Singer, Debbie Ford and Brene Brown.

(Source: watch the video on Oprah.com to see each person on our list answer Oprah's question, *"How would you define God?"*)

http://www.oprah.com/own-super-soul-sunday/How-Do-Top-Spiritual-Thinkers-Define-God-Video

I have added a "Powerful Question" after each definition of God. Use the powerful question to open your own spiritual perspective. Make it meaningful for yourself and to go deeper into your awareness.

Enjoy the process!

How do our present-day spiritual thinkers define God?

Deepak Chopra: "The evolutionary impulse of the universe. God is infinite creativity, love, and infinite compassion and caring."

Powerful Question:

What would your life look like if you were expressing infinite creativity, love, compassion and caring?

Caroline Myss: "God is law. Total mystical law. Because law is the nature of the universe. It's the order of things. It's universal, and the negotiation principal with mystical laws is prayer."

Powerful Question:

What spiritual laws do you live by and how does that show up as prayer?

Marianne Williamson: "An all-encompassing love that is the source of all, the reality of all, and the being through which I am."

Powerful Question:

What is in the way of being all-encompassing love?

Wayne Dyer: "The highest place within each of us – it's our divine self."

Powerful Question:

How are you fearlessly expressing your divine self in the world?

Michael Singer: "The SOURCE of you."

Powerful Question:

How can fearlessness allow you to be "Sourced" in all that you do?

Debbie Ford: "An energy, it has no denomination, no judgements, it has an energy that when we are connected to it we know why we are here."

Powerful Question:

Who would you be if you no longer judged yourself?

Brene Brown: "SPIRITUALITY is a deeply held belief that we're inextricably connected with each other by something greater than us. The "something greater" is rooted in love and belonging. We will never be free from suffering until we are ALL free from suffering, which makes it our job to do something about it."

Powerful Question:

How can you get out of your own way and live fearlessly for the highest good of all?

ELEMENT #1:
Personal Leadership

PERSONAL LEADERSHIP	**BOUNDARIES**	**COMMITMENT**
CHOICE	**PROJECTION**	**INTEGRITY**
SURRENDER	**FORGIVENESS**	**ACCEPTANCE**
INTUITION	**PRESENCE**	**HONORING SELF**

You were born into fearlessness, it's the world that may have taught you to fear. –Robin Sharma

Look for ways that leadership shows up in your life. What mindset would you have as a leader? Perhaps you would be more confident.

Perhaps you would let go of your concern for what others think and let your own light shine brighter.

There might be new ways for you to begin relating to yourself and others from a leadership perspective, one that has you making fearless choices.

Defining leadership on a personal level is a powerful step. Begin forming your personal list of beliefs about your potential as a leader in your own life and with others.

Leadership Beliefs

Notice your thoughts, attitudes and perceptions about your own leadership and the leadership you see in others.

The goal is to become fully aware of your beliefs so you can chose which ones support the level of leadership you want to cultivate and express. The focus is on overcoming beliefs that are limiting or distracting.

EXAMPLES OF LEADERSHIP BELIEFS:

I live in balance and on purpose by serving self and others.

I take a stand for your authentic self.

I deepen my relationships to manifest joy, fulfillment and trust.

I contribute to the world by using my gifts and talents.

I am willing to let go of mediocrity.

I create extraordinary results by living with purpose and passion.

I demonstrate integrity based on what matters most.

Your path of Fearless Living is ongoing and always changing, just as leadership is an ongoing development and expression. Look for milestones to acknowledge as you take on new leadership qualities and find ways to express them.

Acknowledge the measurable steps you take as you make progress defining your leadership.

Personal Leadership Qualities

When your leadership is fully expressed, what QUALITIES do you notice in yourself?

As you take ownership of your leadership, you begin expressing certain qualities more and more. Become aware of your top three personal leadership qualities and make a commitment to expressing them to the best of your ability. Be aware that leadership qualities change and expand along your path.

How would you describe someone demonstrating Personal Leadership?

They strive for excellence versus perfection.

They are committed to the highest form of relationship, known as "passionate service".

They take the highest perspective, known as "thinking outside the box."

They take 100% self-responsibility for all personal thoughts, words and actions.

They have the emotional intelligence to manage others along their path.

They connect with others from empathy and intuition in order to make progress.

They are visionaries – seeing the big picture first and leading from there.

They embrace their fears.

They are informed rather than activated by everything around them.

A Perspective on Personal Leadership

A student in the *Fearless Living* Leadership Training describes her "favorite leader" in terms of qualities and beliefs:

"Leading by example is so the strongest thing Debbie and any of the students can do. Debbie is a guide and a teacher in the purest sense. She is along for the journey to support, question and examine with us as her students.

Debbie never talks about anything that she is not, or has not done. She shares vulnerably and gets the support when she needs it. She embodies strength and courage. She does this by not always being strong and brave. Being accepting is huge as a leader. To accept is to love all parts of us, even the parts we don't deem acceptable.

I feel fully accepted by Debbie's leadership as I know she has had to embrace and love all parts of her to be where she is today."

-Samantha M.

Powerful Questions

What would you want others to say about YOUR leadership?

What qualities would you want to be known for as an influencer?

"Sailing the Stormy Seas."

Do one thing that scares you every day. – Eleanor Roosevelt

It was 1975, still just a kid at 23, and having the time of my life being married. My husband and I decided we wanted to learn how to sail, and ended up enjoying it. We both loved experiencing the power of the wind and the feeling of being powerless over it.

We bought ourselves our first sailboat, a 16 foot Hobiecat, and sailed it almost every weekend during the summer months.

The two of us felt really confident and assumed that we could qualify ourselves as experienced sailors. We figured if we could sail our Hobiecat successfully, then we could sail any boat. Oh boy, little did we know.....

Our sailing arrogance had us determined to go to the next level and go on a bareboat sailing trip. Simply put, bare boating is when you rent a sailboat and you crew the boat yourselves.

Our crew consisted of me, my husband and two other of our college friends who also loved sailing. Fortunately, Sully, one of the four, was more experienced and knew how to use a sextant, so we figured we had everything we needed to sail around the world.

Our plan was to sail from Ft. Lauderdale to the Bahamas. Sounded good to me. Let's do this, it should be fun! I suppose I could say my naiveté masked any fears I may have had because I didn't think twice about participating.

Our plan was to leave in the evening, because Sully said it was the best choice. Sure, I thought. I imagined he knew what he was talking about because the rest of us didn't have a clue talking about because the rest of us didn't have a clue how to sail on the ocean.

The night we were scheduled to depart, a huge storm was predicted with high winds. It was definitely not advisable for sailing.

Now I'm here to tell you I was never a night person, even as a teenager, so the thought of leaving at night would not have been my first choice. I'd rather be snuggled up in bed by 9 pm.

That night we met to consider whether or not to wait till the storm passed. Absolutely NOT they said! We can do this! At 23 years old, we felt that nothing could stop us and nothing would happen to us.

The storm was already starting to rear its ugly head. I started to become afraid. Over 10 foot waves were predicted, heavy rain and strong winds. Now who in their right mind would go sailing in that kind of weather, especially at night? There I was, surrounded by three strong men, so why should it be me to back out?

I went back and forth in my mind trying to decide if I should stay and then fly later to the Bahamas to meet up with them. I was very close to making that choice. Instead, I chose not to trust my gut and went anyway. It was more important that I not be weak or needy versus honor what I knew I should not have done. If my parents had only known!

We take off and it's already rockier than any of us could handle. Sea sickness set in, Sully was in the helm, and the rest of us were puking over the sides of the boat till there was nothing left. No talk of turning back!

I was already feeling depleted and only got sicker. The worst thing to do when you are sea sick is to go down below deck. There I went; down below, because it felt safe. Well, that didn't last long because I needed to heave once again, so back up on deck I came.

The waves were well over 10 feet high. That may not seem like a lot, but when you are on the ocean and you look up and see waves above you, that's high! I have never, ever been more afraid in my entire life. I know everyone else was scared too.

Because of the incredible storm, we lost our bearings. Well, let me tell you what a feeling that was! Sully was unable to get a reading from the sextant and the storm took us so off track that we were completely lost. On top of that, the bilge pump stopped working and we lost our compass! We were taking on water, with no idea where we were and all 4 of us were sea sick. Oh, how I wanted to be tucked away in my bed! All those stories you may have heard about the Bermuda Triangle; I'm pretty sure we were right there!

So here we are, the 4 of us lost at sea....for what seemed like forever, sea sick, soaking wet, scared and with no contact with the outside world. I really don't remember all the details because my fear was so intense, it was all I could do to simply breathe.

For the first time in my life and I pray it was the last time, I seriously considered jumping ship because my fear was so strong, I was so sick and I never felt so hopeless and powerless. I figured that death would be better option than dealing with this nightmare.

I know the others were thinking the same because we talked about it afterwards. I came really close to following through. I can't even describe how it felt to tell myself that I might be better off ending my life.

We continued to weather the storm for hours and hours and all we could hope for was to be found. Did I forget to mention we had no radio connection? Finally, we spotted an oil freighter. I have never been so happy in my life to see the lights of that ship moving closer to our little 20 footer. "Oh my god! We have been found! Dry clothes, a bed, a shower, food and safety! We are going to be saved!" Not! Due to international port authority policies they could not take us onboard. I once again, felt like jumping ship. The good news was that they were able to give us a reading, which set us on our way. Due to the storm, we had sailed a considerable distance off our intended path, so we had a long way to go.

Not too much longer after we were "saved," the storm passed and the rest of the trip was smooth sailing. Once we landed, we found an inexpensive hotel room, showered, changed from salty clothes to dry, slept and resumed our sailing itinerary. The remainder of the trip was fantastic.

What a lesson! By not trusting in myself, I nearly died! By trying to be something I wasn't, I nearly died. By not honoring myself, I nearly died. By trying to act tough, I nearly died.

All of those reasons were reasons based in fear. Had I been courageous and done what I knew was best, this never would have happened.

At the time, I was not aware that my choice was from fear. I unconsciously went along with the crowd. My deeper fears in life were reflected back to me by the fears I faced during the storm! So many insights and revelations.

I was never aware of all the lessons that were available from this experience until I started to explore my internal world and understand the power of fear and how it can nearly kill us! The fear that I suppressed showed up for me a hundred times over.

As I look back on my "Fearful Storm", I now understand three life-changing lessons I received:

1. Fear is there to be embraced, and acted on in a way that will be life giving, not life taking.

2. Fear is a message that our soul is calling our attention.

3. Fear is not my enemy if I own it and take the action necessary to move me powerfully forward.

I am grateful for FEAR, a powerful teacher indeed.

ELEMENT #2:
Boundaries

PERSONAL LEADERSHIP	**BOUNDARIES**	**COMMITMENT**
CHOICE	**PROJECTION**	**INTEGRITY**
SURRENDER	**FORGIVENESS**	**ACCEPTANCE**
INTUITION	**PRESENCE**	**HONORING SELF**

To me, fearless is not the absence of fear. It's not being completely unafraid. To me, fearlessness is having fears. Fearless is having doubts, lots of them. Fearless is acting in spite of those things that scare you to death. – Taylor Swift

Setting and maintaining personal boundaries is an act of self-care and self-responsibility. A boundary is a statement or an agreement for what is acceptable and what is not acceptable in the situation or relationship.

Setting a boundary as a structure to hold your values in place is a powerful way to be responsible for yourself.

Take the perspective that boundaries are a statement FOR something you want or value, rather than a statement AGAINST something you do not value or want.

When we say "NO" to something, we really are saying "YES" to something else. Are you willing to set boundaries as positive statements?

What boundaries would you set to model positive leadership to others? Notice the area of your life where you most need to demonstrate your fearlessness. What boundary would support you?

The biggest obstacle in the way of setting and maintaining boundaries is the fear of the outcome. Being afraid of confrontation, being made wrong and the fear that it won't work will never support you in getting your needs met within yourself or in any relationship.

You must have a new level of self-worth and confidence to create new outcomes with boundaries, knowing that there most likely WILL be resistance.

Doing this work is important in order to set AND maintain your boundaries. If they are not consistently applied, the old behaviors will re-emerge.

Beliefs about Boundaries

Notice where you are coming from when you consider boundaries and how they fit or don't fit into your life and relationships.

Perhaps you anticipate the resistance or rejection of your boundaries. Maybe your self-doubt takes over and you feel uncertain of the value. With practice and success on your side, you begin to feel confident and empowered.

What happens when you communicate your boundaries? What happens when you receive boundaries from others?

EXAMPLES OF BELIEFS ABOUT BOUNDARIES

My boundaries are about making sure my needs are met.

Boundaries give others a clear definition of what I will tolerate and what I will not tolerate.

Effective boundaries require ongoing maintenance.

Maintaining boundaries can be easy and effortless.

Boundaries turn into ongoing negotiations what will work and what will not work.

When my boundaries are strong, I have room for peace and serenity.

By setting positive boundaries, I support myself with compassion.

Boundaries send a message that you value yourself and the relationship.

Boundaries are just words.

Successful Boundary Qualities

See the value of boundaries from the perspective of being a vibrant leader. You are demonstrating your leadership THROUGH your boundaries.

You must first start with clarity in yourself. You must be clear on your own boundaries, and most importantly WHY you are setting a particular boundary. Each boundary sends a message about your values and priorities.

Be willing to see the bigger picture when it comes to your boundaries.

How would you describe someone who is demonstrating Successful Boundaries?

They have a personal clarity with others.

They understand their own needs.

They are a combination of compassion and fierceness regarding others.

They invite others into a deeper connection or expression.

They enjoy freedom and confidence.

They exhibit confidence and self-assurance (because they have a positive structure to rely on.)

They enjoy healthy, thriving relationships.

They demonstrate creating healthy, thriving relationships and inspire others to do so.

They have self-respect and are respected by others.

The Guest House, by Rumi.

This beautiful poem inspires us to create a broader type of boundary around being resilient with our emotions.

This being human is a guest house.

Every morning a new arrival.

A joy, a depression, a meanness, (A FEAR)

some momentary awareness comes

as an unexpected visitor.

Welcome and attend them all!

Even if they're a crowd of sorrows,

who violently sweep your house

empty of its furniture, still,

treat each guest honorably.

He may be clearing you out

for some new delight.

The dark thought, the shame, the malice,

meet them at the door laughing,

and invite them in.

Be grateful for whoever comes,

because each has been sent

as a guide from beyond.

"Amy is Out of Control!"

I like to joke as a life coach that "Boundaries!" are the answer to just about every challenge.

At first glance, we think being good at setting and maintaining boundaries is all about saying NO to what we don't want, with enough power and confidence to pull it off successfully.

Not so much.

Boundaries are really about saying YES to what does matter. A good boundary supports what you WANT, not simply holding up a stop sign to what you do not want.

Carla has a 22 yr. old daughter, Amy, who just couldn't seem to finish college. She had been paying for tuition and living expenses while Amy was attending out of state. Amy was feeling depressed and anxious, losing focus on her goals. She wanted to return home and get her feet back on the ground.

Carla was happy to be available for this next chapter in their relationship and welcomed having her home to make a new plans. Carla had encouraged Amy for years to seek therapy or other support for her feelings of depression and anxiety. She figured now would be a good time to make that happen.

I noticed a pattern after listening to Carla's story. She asked her Amy to see a doctor about anxiety and take steps forward. Nothing happens. Life goes on. Amy asks for her mom for a cell phone, gas for her car, money for social activities and Carla gave her all she could, which was a sacrifice. Carla asked Amy again to see a doctor and take steps forward. Amy refuses and Carla is feeling incredibly frustrated, powerless and resentful. On and on it goes. . .

Turns out Carla is seriously afraid of holding Amy accountable because this might mean her daughter will reject her, breaking off their relationship.

Yes, Carla had tried setting many boundaries; the kind of boundaries that are clearly stated and the kind of boundaries that ask for action and ways to measure if they are done or not done. However, Carla stayed stuck in her fear. She was afraid that by upsetting her daughter, she might leave home and get in trouble. Her fear prevented her from doing what was in the best interest for both of them.

I suggested setting a boundary with herself instead. Can you stay present with your daughter even when YOU feel anxious about being rejected? What boundary would keep you in your confidence as a parent? What boundary would say YES to your own mental health?

Carla needed to see boundaries differently in order to break her pattern of failure. She needs a boundary that empowers her as a parent versus another boundary that draws a line in the sand for what her daughter should or shouldn't do.

If she courageously set a boundary that she will not compromise herself when her daughter's moods or indulgences come up, they can stay focused on a plan for doctor visits.

If she set a boundary for honoring her integrity rather than easing her short-comings by being wishy-washy . . . a parenting breakthrough was right around the corner for her.

Carla chose to step into her fearlessness and first set a boundary with herself. The internal boundary she set and maintained was to stop herself when she found herself giving her daughter unsolicited advice, to walk away when Amy went into her moods, and to, instead, focus on self-care. Carla began to notice how much emotional energy she was using on trying to fix Amy.

As difficult as it was in the beginning, Carla began to feel more comfortable focusing on herself. She began to exercise, eat better and really focus on what makes her happy.

Carla's confidence began to increase. She felt better about herself, so much that she knew she could set some new boundaries with

Amy. Carla was ready to deal with Amy's resistance, but she also knew that she was doing her daughter a disservice by continuing to tolerate things as they were.

Carla set a boundary that Amy was not happy about, but it worked. Carla let Amy know that she would no longer pay for her cell phone, gas for her car and all the extras, if Amy was not willing to get professional support to deal with her depression. Amy DID NOT want to live without all her luxuries yet she knew she would have to honor her mom's request.

Carla never felt so empowered by her own willingness to set and maintain boundaries. She began to set even more and what she felt was miraculous was that her relationship with Amy dramatically improved over time! Carla raised her standards with herself by respecting herself enough to take new actions. And Amy level of respect towards her mom was beyond Carla's comprehension. They are both much happier and they both now understand the value of boundaries.

ELEMENT #3:
Commitment

PERSONAL LEADERSHIP	**BOUNDARIES**	**COMMITMENT**
CHOICE	**PROJECTION**	**INTEGRITY**
SURRENDER	**FORGIVENESS**	**ACCEPTANCE**
INTUITION	**PRESENCE**	**HONORING SELF**

The enemy is fear. We think it is hate. But it is fear.
- Gandhi

By increasing our awareness about how we embrace or resist commitments, we can strengthen our leadership skills. Without commitment, we lack the foundation for fearless living.

How you show up in one area of your life is always a perfect reflection of how you show up everywhere else. Track your approach to commitment in daily life scenarios and you will discover the basis for how you approach the big commitments in your life.

Commitment Beliefs

Notice what you believe about commitment. Notice your thoughts, attitudes and perceptions about your own commitments, your ability to commit and your comfort level with commitment. Notice the commitment you see in others.

The goal is to become fully aware of your beliefs so you can chose which ones support the level of leadership you want to cultivate and express. Remember to focus on overcoming beliefs that are limiting or distracting because those are all fear based and do not serve your highest vision.

EXAMPLES OF BELIEFS ABOUT COMMITMENT

Commitment to self and others is an act of service.

Commitments are intentions that inspire myself (and others).

My commitments promote my highest intentions and what is best for all involved.

My commitments are authentic when they come from my heart or higher self.

The power of commitment defines a person's character.

My level of commitment creates a corresponding level of possibilities.

As you experience living fearlessly at deeper and deeper levels, the value of personal commitment begins to grow. Look for the power of your own intentions and your commitments to those intentions.

If your truth is to fully express your leadership at a 100% commitment level, what would you choose to be committed TO? It's powerful to commit to your highest leadership qualities.

When you make a commitment to speaking your truth everywhere you possibly can, your personal leadership naturally follows.

Personal Commitment Qualities

What do you notice about a committed person? What qualities come to mind that would support you in being fully committed to fearless living? How do you feel when you are with someone who demonstrates a strong commitment? How do you know they are committed?

How would you describe a person who is 100% Committed?

What they say and what they do are in complete alignment.

Their word is reliable, clear and you trust them because they follow through with what they commit to.

They have a certain passion that flows abundantly.

Being with them feels solid.

They come from a strong foundation, grounded and centered.

They are fully present.

Their commitment supports their passion and purpose.

Powerful Questions

*What are the thoughts and beliefs
that cause you suffering in this area?*

What have you been truly committed to?

A Perspective on Commitment

I want to be fearless in my personal commitment. I say I want to decrease or eliminate sweets from my diet. However, after exploring my beliefs and looking deeper, I can see that I am holding onto a commitment that sugar is more important to me than eating as clean as possible!

I became aware that what I was most committed to was eating sweets! My reality was not in alignment with what I said I wanted, which was to eat cleaner and eliminate sugar.

After spending time getting very clear about how this subconscious commitment to sugar stops me from being 100% responsible for my health and well-being, I can now make a new commitment to eliminate sweets from my diet.

Since then, I have not had sweets. The result: I am empowered, healthier, cleaner and more of a leader.

Our reality, whether we like it or not, shows us the truth as to what we are really committed to.

For example, If I told myself over and over that I was committed to budgeting my spending yet I shopped carelessly and never checked my bank account statements, I am out of alignment with my commitment. By looking at my reality, I get to see that I am not committed to my budget. My operating commitment is instead to overspending and immediate gratification.

A commitment is only valid if it is acted upon, otherwise there's something else that you are committed to. Look at your reality and notice what you are truly committed to.

"Retreating from a Retreat?"

"The question isn't who is going to let me; it's who is going to stop me." —Ayn Rand

Commitment is one of the most powerful tools to support you in living the life of your dreams. And it's also one of the most difficult tools because it requires that you walk the talk, that you prove to yourself and to others that you are trustworthy with your word.

The difficulty arises when what you've committed yourself to doesn't unfold in the way that you imagine. Yet following through with the most difficult commitments are empowering and leave you feeling with more integrity than ever.

My integrity was recently tested in a "partnership" that developed between myself and someone who connected with me on a social media site. We began communicating online and she shared her passion of starting a business of leading retreats. Over the course of several online chats, Skype calls, and emails, we worked together and designed a yoga retreat to be held in Mexico.

I'm always open to the possibility of collaborating with others to share my work in the world, so I proceeded to work with her to create a successful retreat for all.

Once we finalized our retreat plans, I agreed to sign a contract. I made a commitment and I had every intention to follow through with what I agreed to. Yet throughout the relationship up to this point, there were red flags. I came to realize that she had no background in leading retreats, no experience in facilitation and no idea how to run a business.

Per our contract, she was to pay me to co-facilitate the retreat, lead the yoga sessions and various personal growth sessions. Fine. That works for me. That's exactly what I love to do! Her role was to do the marketing and fill the seats at the retreat and lead a few of the sessions during the week. It sounded like an ok plan to me. She advertised that there would be 30 attendees, and she promised me at the time that I could rest assured that she could get at least that many because she recently hired a new marketing team. I was excited and hopeful.

As time went on, the retreat website had little to no traffic. I did my part and posted the event to my list, enrolling one of my dearest, sweetest clients ever.

We ended up with only 2 retreatants, one being my client who I will call Sherry. This was Sherry's first time out of the country, a big deal for her! She registered thinking she would have the opportunity to meet lots of other folks to spend the week with. She was also told by my "partner" that there would be another speaker at the retreat besides myself.

A few weeks before the retreat, I began to wonder what it would be like for Sherry to show up in Mexico only to find that the advertising was false; that it was going to be just her and one other person attending and the 3rd speaker was not going to be there. In retrospect, she told me that had she found this out when she arrived, it would not have been pretty.

So I contacted Sherry a few weeks before departure to let her know what was happening. She was very disappointed and upset that she had not been told previous to this. I agreed with her and acknowledged the fact that this was the reason I wanted to notify her. I wanted to know if she was even willing to go on the trip. Here I am partnering with someone who's not showing up in integrity. It felt unprofessional and I was really angry that I entered into this in the first place, however, I signed the contract and I was committed. I shared Sherry's upset with my "partner," and of course she was not happy that I told her. After lots of mediation on my end, Sherry was given a partial refund on her fee. At least that softened the tone a bit, but it was not a good way for my client to enter into a yoga retreat with this energy.

I could describe several other red flags that went down previous to the trip, yet the bottom line; I signed the contract. I was committed. I went into the retreat feeling very skeptical and nervous about the integrity level of the women who hired me. I expected drama based on the history of this "partnership" thus far, particularly because I had already experienced drama from her from the get go. I knew I'd have to go into it making the best out of it and to support the 2 attendees who deserved a joyful and peaceful experience.

Note to the wise: Meeting someone online is only a partial experience of someone. Once I met her in person it didn't take me more than 24 hours to notice what I was in for. My "partner" did not model a yogic way of life. I began to notice that she was most interested in smoking and drinking versus finding peace and calm. I was horrified.

No more than 2 days into the retreat, I get a knock on my door from her. She came into my room blaming me for being disrespectful, for making the attendees cry, for being unprofessional, and on and on and on. I was stunned! I had no clue what she was talking about. She stated that the staff was complaining about me as well. (Mind you, she had no staff!) I asked her to please be specific with what she was accusing me of and her response was "You know what you are doing. YOU are a professional! You either change your act or leave tomorrow morning!"

I can't describe how shocked I was with what I heard and the way she was looking at me! She continued to accuse and blame me for sabotaging her retreat till finally I stated that she needed to leave my room. She told me to meet her at the front desk in the morning.

Bottom line: she did everything in her power to scare me into leaving so that she would have an excuse not to pay me. (None of the accusations were true. I inquired to the 2 sweet attendees if they were dissatisfied with my facilitating and they were shocked to hear that what was said to me were all life.

She stated: You have 2 choices: You either leave tomorrow or change. You sleep on it. I responded by letting her know that there was no way in the world that I would leave (as much as I wanted to).

I stated that I am here to serve the 2 attendees and that I completely committed to what I agreed to do. I know this is not the answer she wanted to hear. She restated: You sleep on it! I again, told her that my answer will be the same in the morning; that there's nothing for me to sleep on.

The rest of the week was horrendous. I did everything I could to be respectful and serve the attendees to the best of my ability.

From my experience, I believe that she did not like that I was the professional, and the two attendees enjoyed my presence, and she had a hard time with this. She did everything she could for the remainder of the week to be short and disrespectful to me. I responded with kindness.

This was one of the most difficult commitments I ever had to complete because it was incredibly difficult. Yet I did what I said I was going to do. It was a huge lesson. She did not fulfill her end of the contract, which was to pay me what I was due. The week was costly on so many levels.

Commitment comes with a high cost. It cost me my time, my energy and my money, yet the benefit of following through outweighs all of the cost. I made a huge impact on the 2 attendees who, unfortunately, witnessed the disrespect and the abuse I received from my "partner."

Choosing to live fearlessly comes with making commitments that will test your integrity, your willingness to endure whatever adversity you are faced with.

I returned home feeling depleted and made sure I had enough down time to decompress. Still feeling depleted because of all the emotional energy it required for me to make the week as pleasant as possible, I knew I wanted to debrief with my coach. She helped me realize that my week in Mexico was a test; not a test I would have chosen, but one that has reminded me that I can make anything happen, if I'm committed to it. My commitment to the 2 retreat guests reminded me of how much I value doing what is right and best for all involved. It defined my character to myself and to the other 2 guests. Not only was I committed to fulfilling the contract,

I was committed to living fearlessly. My fear could have had me be intimidated by my "partner." My fear could have had me lose my cool in front of everyone. My fear could have me show disrespect and I have to say, I was very tempted.

I would never have guessed that a "Retreat Week" would give me a story about power of commitment? For the gift in all of this, I feel blessed.

Journaling Exercise

What would you be doing if you shifted your life from fear to peace?

Make two columns and fill them with examples about what you do from a place of fear, and what you do from a place of peace. Journaling in this way helps you find clarity and allows you to choose the actions you want.

ELEMENT #4:
Choice

PERSONAL LEADERSHIP	BOUNDARIES	COMMITMENT
CHOICE	PROJECTION	INTEGRITY
SURRENDER	FORGIVENESS	ACCEPTANCE
INTUITION	PRESENCE	HONORING SELF

"Having courage does not mean that we are unafraid. Having courage and showing courage means we face our fears." –Maya Angelou

Having a choice is the ultimate freedom. When we do not have a choice, we are stuck or suppressed. Without choice, we are in victim mode, feeling hopeless and limited. The power to choose is relevant to leadership because true leaders create choice and true leaders invite others to be at choice in every possible way.

Each of the twelve elements contain the component of CHOICE. Begin to own the power of choosing your thoughts, your beliefs, your responses, and your emotional state as you expand your understanding of the twelve elements of Fearless Living.

Having the freedom and space to CHOOSE is your ultimate goal on the path of personal development.

Beliefs about Choice

Notice what you believe about the power of choice. Look for the relationship between making choices that support yourself and the outcomes you have in your life. Perhaps you are highly aware of every choice you can make.

Notice your thoughts, attitudes and perceptions about the choices you make and the power of choice you see when others either make choices from positive or negative positions.

Can you believe that you are always at choice in your life? You may not have a choice over situations, circumstances and how others react towards you, however you are ALWAYS at choice around how you experience all of it!

EXAMPLES OF BELIEFS ABOUT CHOICE

No matter what, I can make choices that support my highest good.

The power of choice is a given, in my life at all times.

My integrity inspires my ability to exercise winning choices.

Knowing I can always be at choice keeps me present to my truth.

Every choice matters, because there really are no big or small choices.

My choices give me the ability to respond versus react.

When I choose fearlessly, I'm living in my highest level of integrity.

As we step into a stronger relationship with the part of ourselves who CHOOSES FEARLESSLY, we naturally discover how our choices truly do effect everything.

QUALITIES OF CHOICE

What do you notice about a person who makes powerful choices? What choices would you make to support being fully committed to fearless living? How do you feel when you are with someone who not only offers great choices, but has an abundance of great choices around them?

How would you describe someone who easily and effortlessly makes powerful choices?

They are confident.

They are free and fluid.

Their energy is evenly distributed among body, mind and spirit.

Their wisdom shines through, feeling as if it comes from experience.

They are comfortable knowing that not all choices please the whole.

Journaling Exercise

What choices are you making that are preventing you from success, confidence and fulfillment?

What is one new choice that you can commit to making this week so that you can move forward or step out of your fear?

Declare your new choice/s. How does it feel to declare new powerful actions?

"I'm Running as Slow as I Can: It's My Choice."

I am always amazed at the wisdom I receive on my runs. Perhaps because it draws me into the moment as does my meditation practice, or maybe because running increases my breathing and brings me focus. We all have learned that BREATH is what brings us into the present moment.

Today I reluctantly layered myself against the cold, because I really didn't want to go out and run in the below freezing temperature, but I knew I'd be happy if I did.

The path that I run on was partially clear. Approximately half of the area was either snow packed, ice packed or melting snow so it was definitely not ideal running conditions. I knew I had to be careful whether I liked it or not.

My preference is to run on clear paths so that I can be in control and focus on my speed, if I choose to do so. But not today. I knew I had to pay attention or I would have ended up slipping on the ice and potentially breaking something.

As my pace varied from my typical jog to almost walking and then to just barely walking, it occurred to me what choice I am making; (or I should say, it occurred to me *what choice I needed to make!*)

My ego pushes me to go faster and run harder. That's not a bad thing unless it takes priority over my overall health and well-being. I realized how much importance I placed on running at a reasonable pace, because then I get to feel productive and successful.

The icy path showed me the best choice I can make is to have a safe run. Had I not run in these conditions, I would miss the insight I needed not solely running but for all areas of my life. This "icy lesson" allowed me to see the metaphor for the ways I choose a faster pace over a more effective and healthy pace.

I eat fast. I think fast. I respond fast. I walk fast. When I want something done, I do it immediately and get it done as soon as possible. I want the same from others. And, oftentimes, these fast choices result in impatience, frustration and aggravation. What if, instead, I allowed myself to treat my life as if I were moving along an icy, snow packed path, where I was forced to move at a pace in support of my highest level of health and well-being?

This means I would have to let go of control! I must realize I cannot always set the pace of how life will unfold for me. I would have to take that "next step" to universal trust and surrender to the path before me.

Because I was forced to slow down and be cautious, the moment allowed me to notice each step. My senses were heightened as I listened to the way the snow made a crunchy sound with each step. I noticed how the sun sparkled on the snow and ice. I noticed the footprints and wondered who had run before me. I noticed. I was fully present and no longer attached to my pace. I stopped checking my phone to see how far I had gone and the length of time that I had been running. None of that mattered. My choice to have a safe run cultivated in me a feeling of exhilaration as I breathed in the cold, clean air.

Safe trumped speed.

When I have enrollment conversations with potential coaching clients I'm asked the same question from almost all of them. "How long will it take me to achieve my vision?" And once they become clients they will ask: "I feel like I should be farther along. Why can't this go faster?"

Our society has somehow trained us to believe that the faster, the better. The sooner you achieve, the more value you have. Fast equals success. We live our lives as if everything were a race. What if instead, we could treat our lives as if we were going out for a run on an icy and snow packed trail? What more could we experience?

How much more present and mindful could we be about the choices we are making? What if, by slowing down, and being present, we could notice every precious moment in our internal world, our external world, and particularly in our relationships?

What would it take to defy our fast paced life, let go of feeling like we must keep up and/or do better than the next person, and trust that we are exactly where we need to be to have the fullest and richest experience that life has to offer....at any speed.

I am committed to reminding myself daily that I am always at choice to slow down, smell the roses and bask in the beauty of all of life.

I'm going to head out today and enjoy my slow run.

I like this choice!

"Is it Always Bad to Listen to Fear?"

On my birthday, I gave myself the gift to sprint full out for the last 50 yards of my run today. It felt like a gift because it reminded me of how blessed I am to turn 62 years old, have 43 years of running and racing behind me and I still get to run!

I say this was a gift to myself, but really it's a gift from God. I can do everything I can to stay healthy, but there's a power so much greater than me that has had me withstand knee, back, shoulder, ankle, wrist, and various other injuries. How often I forget the miracle in the body's ability to heal, endure, regenerate and grow?

It has me realizing the same for my emotional world. I do what I can to heal my emotional world, and I don't know where I'd be if I wasn't equipped to deal with the adversity in my life. But without accessing my higher power, I'd be living in the smallness of my fearful ego.

If I listened to my ego this morning, I would have heard: "You are too old to sprint. You might injure yourself. Quit acting like a kid." I would have denied myself the experience of feeling limitless! Yet I chose to listen to what is true: "You are unstoppable. Go for it! Never give up! You are capable." And it felt great!

My precious son and daughter in law decided 5 years ago, that I was a bad influence on my 3 beautiful grandchildren. They have completely alienated me from any contact at all with them. They have "diagnosed" me as having borderline personality disorder. It's been the most difficult challenge I've ever faced.

I could not have endured had I chosen to listen to my fearful ego. I'd most likely still be curled up in a fetal position as I was when this first happened. The only way I've been able to find any peace in this matter is by listening to that still small voice that tells me to trust, to love and to accept that which I have no control over.

That is the same voice that I heard this morning during my run. I heard that I can endure anything and I can thrive through it and bask in the gift of every situation. For that I have immense gratitude for my physical and emotional health, without question. With God's help, I can do anything and so can you.

Every situation in your life is an opportunity to connect with Source Energy and to bask in the rewards.

My message to you: Every choice you make is either an ego driven choice or a divinely led choice.

You get to choose, yet too often we listen to what is most familiar. The gifts lie in allowing yourself to be divinely guided. This is my most difficult choice because it calls me to step outside of my comfort zone. It calls me to embrace the totality of who I am without judgment. It calls me to love myself and others unconditionally, no matter what the circumstance.

What is it you most struggle with?

Which voice will you listen to? The fear based voice or the limitless, all knowing, powerful you! It's right there! Reach for it! Sprint that last 50 yards and know that you've just begun!

ELEMENT #5:
Projection

PERSONAL LEADERSHIP	BOUNDARIES	COMMITMENT
CHOICE	PROJECTION	INTEGRITY
SURRENDER	FORGIVENESS	ACCEPTANCE
INTUITION	PRESENCE	HONORING SELF

"The more you are motivated by love, the more fearless and free your action will be." – Dalai Lama

Projection is a fascinating phenomenon. It is an involuntary transfer of our own unconscious behavior onto others, so it appears to us that these qualities actually exist in the other people.

When we have anxiety about our emotions or unacceptable parts of our personalities, we attribute these qualities - as a defense mechanism - to external objects and other people.

For example, when we have little tolerance for others, we are likely to attribute the sense of our own inferiority to them.

There's always a "hook" that engages us into the act of projection. We see an *imperfect* quality in other people which activates an aspect of ourselves that wants our attention.

Whatever we don't own about ourselves we project onto other people.

Bestselling author Debbie Ford teaches us,

"We see only that which we are. I like to think of it in terms of energy. Imagine having a hundred different electrical outlets on your chest. Each outlet represents a different quality.

The qualities we acknowledge and embrace have cover plates over them. They are safe: no electricity runs through them. But the qualities that are not okay with us, which we have not yet owned, do have a charge. So when others come along who act out one of these qualities they plug right into us."

Beliefs about Projection

Notice what you believe about projections. Perhaps you have never considered the source of your triggers with other people's behaviors.

By taking inventory every time you are activated emotionally by someone else's position, you can find peace by owning the part of yourself that needs attention. Take the time to notice your thoughts, attitudes and perceptions about your projections and the projections of others.

When you become more aware of your beliefs about owning your part in an emotional exchange with someone, you can support the level of fearlessness you want to cultivate and express.

The focus is on overcoming beliefs that keep you from using projection in a productive way in your life.

EXAMPLES of BELIEFS ABOUT PROJECTION

When I deny certain traits in myself, I perpetuate the myth that others have something I don't possess.

When I admire someone, I have an opportunity to find yet another aspect of myself.

I can find the ways I attach to others, and turn them around.

It is impossible to see my full potential without doing the work of taking back projections.

Projection separates.

Projection Qualities

As we are becoming more and more willing to stand in our fearless selves, and to take leadership of our life, it's important to notice what happens when we project our limiting beliefs onto others?

How would you describe someone able to overcome the limitations of projection?

They are confident in themselves.

They are detached and see things objectively.

Communicating with them feels authentic and un-edited.

They are not self-absorbed.

They seem to forgive easily.

They experience projection as an opportunity to come to wholeness, non-judgment and acceptance of self and others.

Journaling Exercise

What new actions will I take to integrate and/or eliminate fear-based judgment and projection?

How will I feel by embracing non-judgment and detachment? (Toward self AND others)

A Perspective on Projection

One of my favorite examples of projection is "The Beach Ball Effect" which is about hiding shame through denial. Picture a colorful and large beach ball and how difficult it is to hold it under water.

Hiding your shame is like holding the beach ball down...until that shame 'explodes' and splashes into your face; all due to something you have suppressed and stored in your subconscious. (Example: You blow up because you can't hold it down any longer, or you lie, cheat or sabotage your dignity in any way.)

Imagine standing waist deep in the warm waters of a beautiful lake while your friends surround you. You've got one hand firmly holding the beach ball (your shame) under the water for fear they might "SEE" this shameful side of you. . . and the other hand waving gracefully while you smile about how wonderful everything is. . .

Imagine the large amount of energy you are using to hold that beach ball out of sight! Consider the truth that releasing it is an act of fearlessness, and that when it comes up "in the light" the outcome will be positive rather than a manifestation of your fears.

"Linda's Floating Beach Ball of Shame"

One of my favorite coaching experiences was with Linda who felt messy and out of integrity with her finances. She had created debt and felt embarrassed about it. She made it mean that she was a failure.

When I asked her where the messy part started, she talked about her ex-husband and her anger toward him for the mess he made of their marriage. She blamed him for *"taking me down the road of financial ruin"* as I heard her say more than once.

She ruminated on stories about how awful he was to take advantage of her financial well-being when she came into the marriage. Yes, there was validity to this story, but more importantly she was not owning her part or doing the work to come to terms with her part in what happened around their debt.

Linda was able to realize how the qualities she judged in her ex-husband were the same qualities she had difficulty accepting in herself. Our coaching sessions helped her see that he was simply mirroring the parts of her that most needed her attention.

She was fearless toward stepping into this work, and she made a plan to repay the debt. She began taking consistent actions with integrity, and her financial life improved quickly. Linda was able to release her shame.

Linda's "beach ball of fearful finances" now floats freely in full view and she is able to share her wisdom, experience and compassion for others in her life.

Working with Linda was a gift to me in seeing my own shame, how I suppress my shame, and how it shows up through projection.

When Linda was able to take a stand and say, "I am Fearless", I was able to join with her. Facing our fears is an act of courage, and on an even larger scale, it is a powerful invitation for others to do the same, and reap the same rewards of courageousness.

Linda's story shows that owning her projection is a process that fosters fully accepting herself just as she is. She doesn't have to be victimized by the parts of herself that she deems unacceptable. Instead she can enjoy the colorful beach ball and use it to spread joy to everyone around her.

"She is, According to Ruth, a Self-Absorbed Idiot!"

Ruth was totally caught in a web of anger and resentment over starting a business with a friend that ended in failure. She lost money and she lost a "friend". She wanted to put it all behind her and start a new chapter in her life free from all the negativity and drama coming from her ex-business partner.

She felt like things be going smoothly for a while and then another confrontation would throw her into a tailspin of negative emotions leaving her depleted and doubting herself.

When we first started coaching sessions, she launched into a frantic story about all the ways this woman had trashed their dreams of a successful business with her self-absorbed neediness and constant attempts to be in control of everything, diminishing Ruth's input and expertise.

I had to stop her several times as she went further into the dramatic story-telling about her, focusing on her, pointing her finger at her, which wasn't helping Ruth move forward at all.

I asked her if she was familiar with the human tendency to project our unmet desires, needs or emotions onto someone close to us.

Since talking about that wasn't half as enticing as launching back into her "dramatic speeches about how manipulative and selfish this woman was", she tried to change the subject and continue ranting.

I persisted, further insisting she stop talking about "HER" and start to focus on addressing her own healing and plan to step out of this destructive rut she is in.

*When we are projecting ourselves all over someone else,
it's automatic to deplete our own reservoir of well-being.*

After Ruth understood the power of projection, I got her permission to go deeper into the courage needed to own her part in the relationship. If she can get clear around what she is projecting onto her business partner, she can get clear on letting go and keeping only what serves her pursuit of fulfillment.

I asked Ruth to give me ONE STATEMENT that describes her biggest frustration. She answered, "She is so obnoxious about always wanting HER way and I'm sick of listening to her put me down."

It wasn't easy for Ruth to own any of this for herself. I asked her to break it down into personal statements. "I am obnoxious about always wanting my way." The next segment brought to light Ruth's tendency to be hard on herself. "I am sick of listening to ME put ME down." At first she couldn't agree that these truths were accurate.

I started coaching her by addressing the first statement of "Being obnoxious". I reminded her that she worked diligently for a year behind the scenes at her day job to get ready for starting this business. She too, was being obnoxious about wanting her way.

It just LOOKED differently played out on her own plate. Since Ruth held a lot of guilt about quitting her day job and disappointing her boos, it was hard for her to own that she did what it took to get her own way. Breakthrough on projection!

Now Ruth can start the work of letting go of her guilt, getting neutral with the part of her that knows how to get her own way (rather than suppressing it or holding shame around it) and stop making her business partner wrong. What she CAN DO (productively!) is to start empowering herself instead!

Next we went deeper into her statement about "I'm sick of listening to her put me down!" I coached her to see how this is 100% projection.

Ruth needed to see it on a personal level, and own that she was doing it to herself. The light switch turned on around all the ways she beat herself up for waiting too long to leave the marriage, fighting in front of her young son, and lying to her husband about manipulating their finances to fund making the transition.

Now Ruth can see that SHE is the one tired of her own bottleneck of negativity.

The good news is that this level of awareness sets her free. She can take back the projections. She will know this work is done when she no longer gets triggered into a tizzy about "HER".

The best way to start owning projections is to ask, "Where does that show up for ME?"

Be prepared that your first response might be denial or resistance. What?? Not ME!

Look further by exploring the opposite expression of your projection. For example, I might resist the idea that I'm selfish until I look at an example in my life where BEING SELFISH would serve me better.

If I am giving my power away by pleasing or allowing myself to be manipulated, then I am out of balance and actually need to be selfish in order to heal the problem. If I project my fear of being selfish onto someone else, well, "do the math. . . ." it will never result in a win.

Of course, I took Ruth to her most challenging projection first: Where do the qualities of "manipulative selfish idiot" show up in her life? She first became defensive about being the opposite of those qualities, siting examples of her generous and smart choices. I helped her see that we sabotage our ability to see projections by tooting our own horn to cover up what it might mean to see ourselves in the rawness of our imperfections.

After digging deeper, it came to light for Ruth that SHE was manipulative and selfish during the time she was working her day job and putting time into her business. It also came to light that she is being an "idiot" by not making good choices to take care of her self-esteem instead of wasting her energy trying to make her partner the wrong one.

I challenged Ruth to "own the part of you that is manipulative and selfish." She opened up about the year prior to starting the business when all she cared about was finding the confidence to step out on her own. We began having more conversations about embracing her imperfections and starting to have some FUN with her inner "idiot-self." This lead to her ability to feel neutral during confrontations with her partner. Or if she's lucky, a smile of gratitude for the lessons and gifts from the experience.

Once Ruth took back what she had been projecting, not only did the relationship with herself shift into more compassion and self-acceptance, the relationship with her partner also shifted.

She amazed herself with the way she could interact with her in a completely new way. The tension between them decreased and they began to restore the friendship.

ELEMENT #6:
Integrity

PERSONAL LEADERSHIP	**BOUNDARIES**	**COMMITMENT**
CHOICE	**PROJECTION**	**INTEGRITY**
SURRENDER	**FORGIVENESS**	**ACCEPTANCE**
INTUITION	**PRESENCE**	**HONORING SELF**

"Everything you've ever wanted is on the other side of fear." –George Addair

Our integrity is the foundation of our truth, our core values, and our power. Integrity is perhaps the most powerful quality when it comes to leadership, for without it, there is no power, and without power, there is no leadership.

Who are you really being, when you are 100% in your integrity?

If your INTEGRITY reflects the values you are committed to expressing, then you are absolutely on track. If you notice that you are compromising or abandoning your values, then you just stepped into an opportunity to make an adjustment toward your integrity.

In the big picture, we take both roles – sometimes we are leading and sometimes we are following. There is integrity in each role.

Honoring our INTEGRITY allows us to be in the highest service to self and others.

Beliefs about Integrity

Notice what you believe when it comes to your personal integrity. Check in with the primary areas of your life: Work, Finances, Health, Relationships, Well-Being, and focus on overcoming beliefs that distract you from your integrity.

EXAMPLES OF BELIEFS ABOUT INTEGRITY

I have everything I need when integrity is present.

My personal well-being is ties to my integrity.

My integrity benefits everyone around me.

Integrity is my natural expression.

Integrity requires fearlessness.

INTEGRITY QUALITIES

As you work with the Twelve Elements of Fearless Living, you come into intimate connection with your integrity.

You are seeing how each element effects EVERYTHING, and you are seeing the absolute importance of upholding your integrity inside and out.

Imagine yourself in your fullest expression of the twelve elements. Your personal style shows through. Your energy is fully expressed through your leadership in all areas.

Integrity is the ultimate requirement for this vision to be realized. Imagine that your integrity is the fuel you need to express this vision of your fearless leadership.

How would you describe a person with integrity?

I feel that I can trust them.

They are solid, wise and present.

I feel safe and secure around them.

It's easier to relate openly with them.

They give me permission to be present with them.

They are fearless knowing that their integrity might not please everyone.

They walk their talk.

"From Stuck to Fulfilled."

"Don't be afraid to give up the good to go for the great." – Rockefeller

Several years ago I was in a relationship that had me feeling good, at times, yet never great. I never felt fulfilled by the relationship, and often talked myself into feeling good about it, even though I was completely stuck.

I was doing some part time coaching with families in particular and loving my work. I coached families on the topic on Integrity by defining what matters most in their lives, individually and as a family.

Fear had me stay in a relationship that was out of integrity with what I value. I realized I was afraid, stuck in my fears of leaving a "known situation" and yet, was not doing the work to become clear and take actions.

I worked with my clients to get clear around what they valued, and as they did, they become increasingly aware of where they were in alignment with their values. I helped them see where they were out of alignment with their values. Yet, all the while, I was out of integrity with my relationship.

My own personal journey of stepping out of my fear was just beginning.

We all needed to realize where we are out of integrity by compromising what matters most when we are stuck in fearful thoughts and beliefs.

I remember working with Angie. She became very clear that what mattered most to her was family. We explored what she most valued with her family and she realized she valued honesty, respect, trust and connection.

As I worked with her she came to realize how out of integrity her relationship with her husband and son were because her values were not being expressed and lived.

As we explored her thoughts, beliefs and behaviors, she realized that the lack of respect that she was experiencing was because she was too afraid to request it. She had very little boundaries with her teen age son, Ben, in particular and it resulted in disrespectful language, coming in late and being irresponsible.

Angie was so afraid of setting boundaries with Ben because she didn't want conflict, yet it continued to eat away at her and the connection she felt in her family was nowhere close to what she wanted.

Angie realized she was not living in integrity with what mattered most to her. Angie realized that her lack of integrity was affecting her health and well-being. She also noticed how it was affecting her family's health, well-being and the lack of communication that resulted.

Fear stopped her from doing what was most needed and wanted in a way that would allow her to trust in herself.

The good news is that with the coaching I was supported Angie with, she was able and willing to feel her fear. In her moment of clarity, she was able to use her fear energy and transfer it into courage.

Now Angie is on her way to transformation and stepping into Fearlessness. There I was supporting Angie into fearlessness, all the while, feeling stuck in MY fear!

Soon Angie put boundaries in place, gained respect from her entire family and created an empowering new level of self-trust. By stepping into integrity, Angie became more honest with herself and her family. The results she created by living in integrity, even though they were challenging, scary and sometimes difficult to implement, had her feeling more connected, fulfilled and respected in her family.

During this time, while I worked with Angie and other families to live a life of integrity, I felt like an imposter. My growing level of discomfort lead me to reflect and work with my own coach.

I looked around and noticed that my life seemed to be just fine. I have a beautiful luxurious home. I had all the jewelry and stuff that I ever dreamed of. I had the freedom to do what I wanted like play golf, garden, and play. Life was good, and even though it was definitely not great, I was okay to settle for good.

The day came when I was ready to own the truth: *I was settling by being out of integrity with what mattered most to me, which was TO BE IN INTEGRITY.*

I came to realize that I'm working with my clients about integrity, yet I was in a relationship that was not serving me or my partner. I was waiting for the relationship to change. I was living a fantasy that it would change. I was trying to make it something that it clearly would never be. I spent lots of conscious and unconscious energy convincing myself that I should stay in the relationship because of all the things I had. I was paralyzed in fear.

I took comfort in all the material things I was blessed with. I justified my situation be telling myself things could be worse. I continued to wear the mask of the ideal couple and I did it well. I rationalized, justified and made excuses to myself as to why I should stay in the relationship. It sounded like: "He's not a bad guy. He fills up my car with gas. He might change. I should not let anything bother me because I have a nice home." It went on and on and on....

I did not anticipate how toxic my choice of living out of integrity would be when it effected my health. I suffered with lots of sinus infections, viruses, and was always fighting a cold. Fear was affecting not only my mind, but my physical self as well.

I was so consumed by my fear of leaving that I instead, I put the energy into talking myself into being okay with feeling stuck. I chose to believe that I didn't have to feel a wonderful sense of complete fulfillment. I chose to believe that so many others have it so much worse off than me. I'm really not stuck, I'm really Okay. . . .

Until I decided that I was no longer willing to tolerate mediocrity for myself or for my husband. I decided it was time to completely walk my talk.

I chose to step into fearlessness. The more I was able to see how my clients were out of integrity with what mattered most, the more I was able to see how I was not modeling what I most valued and enjoyed teaching. I became aware of the projections I was making on my clients who were also settling out of fear, and the opportunity that was before me.

Just as with Angie, I had to really get clear around what I was most afraid of and realize how I was allowing my fear to not only affect my life in an unhealthy way, but it was also affecting my partner. Not only was I doing myself a disservice to play small and settle; I was doing him a disservice as well because I could not give him what he wanted in the relationship.

I left the relationship. Yes, I was incredibly scared as I knew I'd have to start from square one by building a business and finding a home. I knew that in order for me to truly support my clients to living a life of integrity, I HAD to model it. I knew I had to face my fears and with the support of my coaches, I did it!

I made the choice to believe that I don't have to feel stuck. I knew I would never experience fulfillment as long as I continued to allow my fears to drive my choices, which I had been doing for much too long. I knew that integrity would allow me to feel clean, to be completely honest with myself and with him and I also knew that by living in integrity I could love him from a much purer space. I felt emotionally liberated by making the choice and then creating the plan to transition.

Choosing integrity in all areas of my life came with challenges. Integrity required that I step out of what I thought was a safe comfort zone. Integrity required that I live my God given purpose so support others by, first and foremost; walking the talk. I was no longer willing to be an imposter because of my fear.

I did it! Making a conscious choice with my fear is the way I can own it and not allow it to have any power over me.

I can't imagine if I had stayed in the relationship. I am grateful for this man and our partnership. Because of him, I learned the lesson of integrity. I learned how to move from stuck to fulfilled. I love him for all of this.

My wish is that he, too has moved from stuck to fulfilled because he deserves it. The miracles that have been created because I believed I could experience fulfillment have been beyond my wildest dreams.

I am eternally grateful for the ability to write a story like this, with my intention to inspire others to step into integrity and moving from stuck to fulfilled.

ELEMENT #7:
Surrender

PERSONAL LEADERSHIP	**BOUNDARIES**	**COMMITMENT**
CHOICE	**PROJECTION**	**INTEGRITY**
SURRENDER	**FORGIVENESS**	**ACCEPTANCE**
INTUITION	**PRESENCE**	**HONORING SELF**

"The greatest act of courage is to be and to own all of who you are – without apology, without excuses, without masks." –Debbie Ford

What if letting go completely and allowing yourself to boldly embrace "not knowing" or "not doing" was the most powerful choice you can make?

Consider that surrender is an act of power. This idea is contrary to common beliefs and experiences of surrender that include vulnerability, weakness and submission. We label these qualities in a negative light, based from a fearful place of losing control. This keeps us from seeing the beauty, the power and the opportunity in surrender, certainly in a positive light. It's fair to say, "To surrender" has negative connotations.

Surrender Beliefs

Notice your thoughts and attitudes toward surrender.

Perhaps you don't connect with this particular WORD. Notice if the word SURRENDER conjures negative or uncomfortable feelings. Do you believe the word surrender means certain things? Try substituting a different word. Use the words "softening" or "allowing" or "leaning into" instead.

Apply these different words and get the full picture of how the SURRENDER plays out for you.

What perceptions do you have when it comes to surrendering in your own life? What capacity for surrender do you see in others?

EXAMPLES OF BELIEFS ABOUT SURRENDER

I can be flexible and present to the moment.

I can tap my inner wisdom with ease.

I can be more flexible with my thoughts and emotions.

I am not distracted by ego/small minded thoughts.

I can step out of fearful or controlling tendencies.

Surrender allows an energy of ease versus effort.

My power lies in surrender.

Surrender Qualities

Imagine your higher self, the part of you completely wise and fully connected to your source. When you see this expression of yourself, how would you describe the quality of surrender that is evident? Perhaps detached, free, flowing, present or fulfilled?

You must define surrender for yourself in an empowering light.

Start by taking inventory of situations or relationships where surrender comes naturally for you. Notice where you see the positive benefits of your ability to surrender in certain areas of your life.

When you bring these into the spotlight, you are able to build and increase your potential to surrender even more.

How would you describe a person expressing the power of surrender?

They are detached.

They have a free flowing way of being.

There is an underlying power about them.

Being with them feels comfortable.

They are present.

They have a high level of self-trust and trust in the universe.

They live their life according to the Serenity Prayer. "God grant me, etc.

Powerful Questions

What areas of your life are easy for you to give, make room, allow, and soften yourself?

In contrast, where in your life is it most challenging or difficult to express surrender?

How much effort does it take to hold on tight?

"Marsha's Courage to Love an Addict."

Marsha adopted her sweet baby boy, Dillon Cole on 8/05/1992. Marsha believes adoption is impossible to describe or truly understand without having the actual experience. She felt an instant connection and unconditional love as soon this sweet baby boy was placed in her arms. She immediately felt, "He's mine!" in that very instant.

Dillon was a wonderful baby. He slept well, was happy and was joyfully active and engaging. He was nothing but an absolute joy in Marsha's life.

When Dillon became an adolescent he started using drugs and alcohol, unbeknownst to Marsha until she started seeing his grades fall, and his behavior dramatically changed.

The challenges Marsha faced with Dillon's behavior continued to worsen. He abused drugs and alcohol throughout his high school years resulting in more failing grades, tardiness, and everything else that goes along with addictive behaviors.

She tried everything to "fix" the situation. She grounded him, took away privelages and rewarded only good behaviors, she coerced, she begged, she diligently helped him with homework, checking in with his teachers on a daily basis, and everything else in the book.

Marsha felt like a hopeless failure. With all her failed attempts to change Dillon's addictive behavior, she became incredibly afraid, powerless and desperate. Marsha was watching someone she loved so dearly destroy his life. It was the most devastating experience she could imagine.

Marsha was a mess, filled with anxiety, sleep deprived and fearful that any moment a police officer would be at her front door. She worried about getting a call from Dillon's teachers saying he was absent. She had never experienced these feelings of powerlessness before in her life.

Now that Dillon was continuously using drugs and getting into more trouble, the level of powerlessness Marsha felt was overwhelming.

"The pain was so great, all I wanted was to save him, fix him, manage him, because then I'd feel like I had some level of control." Marsha was desperately looking for an answer, a miracle, because nothing to this point was effective.

"I can remember endless nights lying awake wondering if Dillon was alive." They were able to enroll him in a school for high risk teens; a place in New Mexico where he could detox and get sober."

Marsha's emotions were layered with sadness, anger, grief, desperation, and yet she also felt a dramatic sense of relief for the ability to sleep at night knowing he was safe at the school, sober, fed and warm.

Marsha had to face knowing that Dillon would always be an addict. Fearful questions pounded through her mind: What will happen when he leaves the school? How will I be able to keep him away from drugs and alcohol? What will I be able to do?

Marsha carried deep shame around feeling like she was a horrible mother, especially as a single mother. She blamed herself and felt convinced that Dillon's actions were a reflection of her parenting.

When I met Marsha, I encouraged her to create a strong support system. Eventually she could acknowledge the shame she was carrying, particularly shame over not being able to fix Dillon's situation. She realized how her shame was destroying her emotional, spiritual and physical well-being, because she was trying to control something she had no control over. She was depleted. Her anxiety level was off the charts. She suffered from depression and felt no joy in her life.

By Marsha's willingness to shift the energy she was spending on trying to fix her son, onto her inner world, healing began.

Our coaching sessions helped Marsha find her inner guidance and clarity so she could see what she had no control over. She began to feel hopeful knowing that by taking responsibility around what she CAN control, possibilities would arise.

By learning how to surrender, without resignation, Marsha felt a sense of relief. Surrender felt very unfamiliar to her. She immediately felt like she wasn't doing enough by letting go. She realized how attached she was to managing Dillon's life and the impact it was making on both of them.

As Marsha surrendered to the situation, she began to notice that in that surrender was where her power resided. She accessed the power to shift her perspective and notice the fear based thoughts that were making things worse. She accessed the power of her faith and her ability to experience the situation from a place of courage; the courage to surrender.

She needed to embrace her biggest fear: That Dillon would die. She needed to surrender to any and all outcomes; and this scary place is where she can began to find her courage.

Marsha began embracing fearlessness to the best of her ability, knowing her healing journey was one small step at a time. She called on her courage to become the mother she IS rather than the mother she thought she needed to be.

"It takes a tremendous amount of courage to trust that there was some greater purpose in this nightmare." Marsha always knew deep down that it was all up to her to be brave and move forward.

That meant Marsha needed to let go of making this situation mean anything about her personally. It meant she could no longer hide out and pretend that she was ok.

Marsha took charge! She started sharing her experience with others and felt a release. Her favorite quote became, "The truth will set you free." She celebrated every milestone as it happened.

She realized that she does have power, maybe not the power to manage Dillon's life, but the power to manage her own. Things started to shift for the better.

Marsha is able to use the gifts and wisdom she learned from her shame to help others in similar situations. She became a social worker and began working with high risk teens. She taught classes and worked in group homes, offering support, healing, connection and wholeness.

Marsha's power showed up by using her "nightmare," to aid others in their shame.

Marsha speaks from her heart, "My journey with Dillon required vulnerability as it still does. I've come to know that vulnerability is the most accurate measurement of courage. My vulnerability opens a space for others to be vulnerable as well and that's where the healing starts."

Marsha's story illustrates how we see vulnerability as weakness. Yet, vulnerability is only a weakness if we decide so. The power lies in the surrender, letting go, being vulnerable and embracing the shame we feel.

ELEMENT #8:
Forgiveness

PERSONAL LEADERSHIP	**BOUNDARIES**	**COMMITMENT**
CHOICE	**PROJECTION**	**INTEGRITY**
SURRENDER	**FORGIVENESS**	**ACCEPTANCE**
INTUITION	**PRESENCE**	**HONORING SELF**

"The greatest gift of forgiveness is that we free ourselves." -Debbie Ford

The power of forgiveness is an untapped resource in our lives. Imagine releasing your resentments, your disappointments, even your shame with a loving intention to heal through forgiveness. If freedom is truly the result of forgiveness, we must start with self-inquiry.

It's important to look inside for the sources of your anger toward others or toward yourself, and to see where you can bring these challenges to the surface and make room to forgive all of it.

Being on this path of Fearless Living means that your inner wisdom is already in the spotlight, so you are well on your way toward freedom, healing and the joys of forgiveness.

BELIEFS ABOUT FORGIVENESS

Notice the beliefs you hold around forgiveness. What comes to mind about forgiving yourself, forgiving others and valuing forgiveness above all?

Perhaps forgiveness comes easy for you because you always see that it's bringing peace into your world. Or maybe you hold grievances that feel unforgiveable and struggle to find ways to begin forgiving. Maybe you don't see the value of forgiving in certain situations.

Maintaining positive beliefs about forgiveness allows us to hold the space for others to forgive and to be forgiven. If you believe in the power of forgiveness, your process is naturally easier.

By removing the fear based belief that "I can't" forgive, will unleash the negative energy that lies within you.

Forgiveness, ultimately, is not about the other. Forgiveness is an inside job that fosters healing, no matter what behaviors you have experienced or continue to experience in someone else.

Forgiveness does not mean you must tolerate an unhealthy behavior. Forgiveness offers you the opportunity to shift your perspective and set healthy boundaries that will move you powerfully forward.

EXAMPLES OF BELIEFS ABOUT FORGIVENESS

Forgiveness is possible in ANY situation.

Forgiveness is a gift to myself.

Forgiveness is an ongoing project.

To forgive is the ultimate gift TO MYSELF.

Forgiveness allows you to take back any power you have given over to anyone.

Forgiveness and boundaries go hand in hand.

When opportunities for forgiveness come up in your life, notice what choices work well, and continue to apply them. Choices that don't work well are taken as lessons that will make room for healthier choices in the future.

The need to forgive is a result in making something or someone wrong.

Fearless Living teaches us to turn judgment into learning, therefore leaving no need to forgive.

Forgiveness Qualities

Imagine being completely free of all grievances, past hurts or anything you are unable to forgive. Imagine this part of yourself as an angel, or being of light. From this view, how would you describe the quality of forgiveness available to you? Perhaps abundant, love-filled or an energy of extreme compassion?

How would you describe someone who can easily forgive?

They are "without a resentful bone in their body."

They are openly accepting toward others.

They have an inspiring level of self-esteem.

Their capacity for love is abundant.

They can easily shift from judgment to acceptance.

Fearless Living includes being open at the deepest level, to the concept that there really is nothing to forgive.

If forgiveness feels difficult, it's because there is still judgment over a situation or person. Having the skills to shift one's perspective from judgment into complete acceptance removes the need for forgiveness.

Forgiveness and acceptance go hand in hand.

Acceptance is the catalyst to forgive. In order to let go of suffering about any sort of "wrong" doing, the element of forgiveness allows us to completely accept our reality just as it is, (versus arguing with reality). We can realize there is nothing to make wrong or to make right. This is true forgiveness.

"Enjoying the Buffet of Life"

"I finally realized that being grateful to my body was key to giving more love to myself." –Oprah

Karen came to me for support over her lifelong frustration with her weight. She tried every diet in the book, only to lose and gain back more than she started out with. She felt powerless over her yo-yo cycle of losing and feeling good temporarily and then gaining all the weight back that she lost, which took her back into the cycle of self-sabotage and low self-esteem.

She was angry at herself, and at everyone and everything that triggered her cravings. Her self-esteem was at an all-time low, and she knew something had to shift or she would never find peace.

Karen told me that she had been overweight her entire life and always wanted to be thin. She felt like an outsider because she didn't feel "normal." She convinced herself that there was something wrong with her, that she was unacceptable and unlovable. As a child, these self-limiting beliefs were unconscious. She was not aware that she was telling herself that she was not good enough, but her behavior reflected these thoughts.

The shame she felt was incredibly deep, feeling as if she could never be like everyone else. So to hide her shame, she did everything she could to get the love and attention she wanted by seeking perfection in everything she did.

Karen got good grades in school, she became a people pleaser so she could feel accepted, she was the good daughter who never disobeyed her parents and Karen made sure the world could see her as perfect. However, she believed she was far from perfect. She lived her life in self-judgment, making herself wrong for her weight. The more she judged herself, the more she ate. The more she ate, the more she judged. It became a vicious cycle that left her feeling powerless, resigned and depressed.

Addressing the emotional component of eating is THE most difficult of all. You can make healthy choices with your food and have an exercise program that will support your goals, yet if you do not explore the emotional component, those sneaky, seductive sabotaging thoughts and beliefs will sneak back into your life and take you back to those unhealthy patterns of your past? Why? Because old beliefs are most familiar and the ego loves familiar. The ego likes to feel in control by knowing the outcome of our choices. Karen's ego was keeping her stuck in her telling her: "You can't do this! You are a failure! You are not lovable, acceptable and you are a loser." As much as Karen wanted to believe otherwise, that old familiar story had such a powerful gravitational pull, it left her powerless and ready to give up.

And then Karen learned the concept of Forgiveness. Forgiveness was the tool that turned her life from stuck to unstuck, and from powerless to powerful. Forgiveness taught Karen that feeling like a failure was a story that she made up about herself that wasn't true. She came to realize the power of her self-judgment and how it affected the way she relied on food for comfort. Her anger had her overeat and become sedentary. Karen realized how committed she was to believe she was a loser. She was completely committed to judging herself and the impact it had on her internal world. Her first "aha" moment was the realization that if she could be 100% committed to feeling like a failure, that she had the power to use that same level of commitment towards being a success.

I guided Karen with some deep forgiveness processes. She began by really digging deep into the parts of her internal world that she was making wrong: judgmental, pushy, stubborn, lazy, selfish, not good enough, different, too fat, and several other qualities that emerged as she continued the process. Her aha moments was when she realized that all of these qualities that she mentioned were exactly the words she heard as a child. She was bullied and made fun of for being overweight. She "adopted" these qualities because this was who she believed she was! Karen was able to see how unwilling she was to forgive herself for making all of these parts of herself wrong. She noticed that she, too, was bullying herself! She perceived herself as flawed and had no idea that by letting go of the self-judgment, she could liberate herself from her internal prison!

Forgiveness, Karen soon learned, is a process. It's not a one-time deal. Yet Karen was willing to begin the process of unwinding all the ways she had been judging herself even as a young child.

Karen's first step was to begin getting in touch with her internal world; which resulted in allowing herself to be completely present when she felt judgmental, pushy, stubborn, lazy, etc. What you feel, you heal, and she focused her attention on her healing process. What she realized is that she was using food to numb herself from feeling all those feelings she was making wrong. She felt like she was in a hamster wheel. No wonder why she felt emotionally depleted!

We did lots of work around letting go of judging all those parts of herself. Karen really felt the impact it was making on her life. By giving herself permission to observe her feelings, she instantaneously felt the power she had to make a new choice. She realized that she no longer had to feel victimized by her feelings; that she was capable of doing something different with her self-judgment and let it go. For the first time in a very long time, Karen felt hope; hope that she could achieve her goals.

With her continued commitment to her internal world, she took time daily to journal around the emotions that triggered her to make unhealthy choices. She noticed the impact of those emotions and implemented new structures to shift her feeling of failure into feelings of empowerment. She forgave herself for all the ways she had made herself wrong for so many years. She forgave herself for all the choices she made that had her so angry and resentful at herself. And she forgave herself for trying to be perfect.

The more she forgave herself, the more empowered she felt and the more empowered she felt, the more motivated she became to taking actions that supported her weight goals. The pounds began to come off and it happened without any trendy diet. She began an exercise program that was realistic. She started tracking her weight and learned to forgive herself when the scale went up. Karen let go of the judgment around the results and trusted that if she did whatever it took to achieve her goals, it would happen.

By accepting what she considered flaws, she told me that she experienced her divinity, her essential self who is unstoppable, limitless and successful.

Not only did her internal world shift through having a daily self-forgiveness practice, she lost 70# and is still moving towards her ideal weight. Karen told me that she's never felt so much compassion for herself, and what's more is that the compassion she feels is also felt towards everyone in her life. Through forgiveness, Karen has experienced miracles for herself and her unstoppable energy is palpable. Because of her commitment to forgiving herself, and achieving ideal weight, Karen feels more purposeful than ever. She intends to support others on their weight loss journey creating a ripple effect with the powerful tool of forgiveness.

ELEMENT #9:
Acceptance

PERSONAL LEADERSHIP	**BOUNDARIES**	**COMMITMENT**
CHOICE	**PROJECTION**	**INTEGRITY**
SURRENDER	**FORGIVENESS**	**ACCEPTANCE**
INTUITION	**PRESENCE**	**HONORING SELF**

"I am afraid. Yet fearless. For fearlessness is not the absence of fear, but the bravery to do it anyway." – Natalie Ladik

Accepting ourselves, accepting others, accepting our circumstances, accepting the perfection of our lives. . . . This process is ongoing and it is always present.

We have the ability to either accept or to resist anything in any moment.

Feel into the difference between acceptance and resistance as you look into the areas of your life. Acceptance can be a choice or a perspective you can use to gauge yourself, as you use it to choose peace and harmony rather than the struggle it takes to overcome resistance.

Allow yourself to open up and completely ACCEPT the truth and presence of everything as it is in your life.

Acceptance Beliefs

Notice your level of self-acceptance. If you believe in yourself (acceptance), then being fearless is an easy choice. If you believe (accept) your power, you are positioned for great outcomes.

You must work to diligently accept all undeveloped parts of yourself as you grow. You must allow, open up to and integrate what serves you, and you must let go of what doesn't serve you.

Perhaps the greatest examples of leadership are grounded in ACCEPTANCE. To practice the power of acceptance, we will fully use our ability to be present with an open heart. This perspective shows the quality of ACCEPTANCE as a beautiful connection.

EXAMPLES OF BELIEFS ABOUT ACCEPTANCE

I can allow situations to unfold.

My intuition supports my acceptance at all times.

I can always find my way to an accepting place.

Acceptance allows me to eliminate excuses, denial and aversion and has me step into all that is real.

Acceptance Qualities

Imagine the greatest version of yourself, including the part of you completely resilient and fueled by your connection to source. When you feel into this expression of yourself, how would you describe the quality of acceptance that is evident?

This perspective allows you to imagine your open heart and out-stretched arms with an abundant capacity to hold everything with love.

How would you describe a person who expresses Acceptance?

They are open.

I can sense their heart energy.

There is an absence of fear, manipulation and anxiousness.

I feel a sense of possibility with them.

It's easy to engage with them.

"Touchy-Feely Superpowers"

Have you been told you are "too emotional?"

Too touchy-feely?

In my experience of these labels, the message is that I "should" be different; that I "should" not be as expressive as I am.

The urban dictionary defines touchy-feely as, "very emotionally open. A touchy-feely person wants to share their thoughts and emotions and have others share theirs. Touchy feely information is personal, sensitive, reflective, and sentimental, and occasionally refers to religious content/ideas. Typically has a negative connotations."

What? Negative connotations?

It seems there is more acceptance for those who live from the neck up – or in their thoughts. We are taught that using our head (thoughts) in dominance over our feelings is more "socially acceptable."

What if we could perceive our emotions not as weaker or less desirable, but instead as responses that work in tandem with the mind?

Notice how the power of acceptance is at work, giving us the opportunity to tap our fullest potential as human beings.

The truth is, our emotions DO work in tandem with our thoughts. Our cognition and our emotions are dynamic, interactive and interdependent. Cognitions and emotions work together to contribute to our activity and behavior. Most of the time this happens automatically and at a subconscious level.

The challenge is to increase our awareness of the emotions that arise in any given moment so we can make choices and decisions based on our physiological response to the situation at the moment.

When we allow ourselves to access our touch-feely side, the transformation occurs. We are ACCEPTING our fullest capacity and ability to create what we want in life.

Accepting the harmony and equality of our mind/emotions requires a willingness to let go of any beliefs we have about our feelings. It is only our conditioning that keeps us believing we cannot show our emotions, especially when we come from situations in the past where we were judged for our feelings.

Notice where you hear these demands: "Don't Cry!" "You are too emotional." "What a baby." "Be Happy!"

It's no wonder why we feel 'safer' in our head. Being fully expressed emotionally means you might be judged as a failure.

Accepting the truth and beauty of your emotional self can set you free from these fears. Are you willing to become more consciously aware of what you are feeling? Perhaps it might feel scary to give yourself permission to feel angry, lonely, bored, resentful, or any other emotion you judge as negative/wrong.

Bringing awareness to your feelings and completely letting go of judging or managing them is where you step into Fearless Living.

We were not put on this earth to have a thought; we are here to have an experience and that can only be had by being attentive to the messages that are available in every moment. Once you allow yourself to feel whatever is there, then you are no longer imprisoned by it.

Reflection Exercise for Self-Acceptance

Use this exercise to develop awareness about your emotions. This is the key component of self-acceptance.

Find some quiet and stillness.

Spend a few moments where you have no distractions and give yourself permission to feel whatever is there; whether it be anger, sadness, fear, etc.

Begin to consider all the behaviors that are driven by that feeling in a way that doesn't serve you.

(Example: My anger has me lash out at my husband. My fear of success has me overeat.)

Now go back to that emotion and just be with it. Notice what shifts.

If you feel resistant to the emotion that arises, allow yourself to simply feel the resistance.

Allowing yourself to be completely present will train your mind (mind and emotion working in tandem) to make new choices that will allow you to be fully expressed and maybe even be labeled as "touchy feely!"

Ask yourself: What does this emotion want me to know right now? And: How can I give myself complete acceptance when I feel this emotion?

Bask in the knowing that your emotions are messages, asking your mind to work together to live authentically, passionately and completely self-accepting!

ELEMENT #10:
Intuition

PERSONAL LEADERSHIP	BOUNDARIES	COMMITMENT
CHOICE	PROJECTION	INTEGRITY
SURRENDER	FORGIVENESS	ACCEPTANCE
INTUITION	PRESENCE	HONORING SELF

"Beware: I am fearless, and therefore powerful."
-Mary Shelley

Inner knowing is accessible to everyone at all times. "What does your GUT FEELING tell you about that?" We are aware and in touch with our intuition more than we realize.

Perhaps the skills of leadership and living fearlessly are based in remembering to connect with internal wisdom, and using the power of our intuition.

Imagine your intuition like a "calm mountain lake" – it is deep, reflective, contained and it is always present. Your intuition is always waiting to be accessed and trusted.

Beliefs about Intuition

Trusting our intuition is the powerful choice. This choice activates our self-trust, resourcefulness and our independence.

Notice if you hold any "dis-beliefs" about your intuitive abilities. Perhaps you doubt or abandon your intuitive side out of fear? Notice where you are most fearful in your life and you will likely find the greatest need to trust in your inner knowing.

EXAMPLES OF BELIEFS ABOUT INTUITION

I deeply value and honor the human being that I am.

I am a very perceptive and intuitive person.

I trust myself and value my inner wisdom.

My intuition is an abundant resource.

My intuition is a universal intuition, that when listened to, serves the highest good.

Trusting your own intuition is an act of power. Notice the cycle that starts when you access your intuition: connecting with your internal wisdom, trusting in yourself, expressing your truth with wisdom and harmony.

The opposite of intuition is self-doubt. In fearless living, anything surrounded by self-doubt is a sabotage. It's useful to activate your intuitive energy as a way to overcome self-doubt.

Too often we allow our fear to get in the way of accessing our intuition because our intuition speaks the truth. Being fearful of what is true keeps us in the hamster wheel of denial, excuses and fear driven thoughts.

Intuition Qualities

Have you noticed that intuition is intriguing? We are naturally curious about it. Perhaps expressing this quality is your invitation to be more playful?

Imagine having a repertoire with your inner world that automatically includes intuitive expression to its fullest capacity.

How would you describe someone with a well-developed intuition?

They have a multi-faceted awareness

They are emotionally self-sufficient

I imagine them seeing in the night or the dark.

Preservation of innermost feelings.

They are good at being still and reflective

They are free from entanglements.

Their inner knowing allows them to make choices that support everyone.

"Thank you, Jenny's Intuition!"

Jenny was starting a new chapter in her life as a single mom with a small daughter. She was determined to create a fresh start for herself with her own business.

She decided to attend a weekend retreat focused on personal growth, since the last few years of challenges in her family seemed to have zapped her spirit and exhausted her energy.

She was inspired at the retreat to hire a life coach to help her stay focused on her new growth.

In my first session with Jenny, she talked about her current work situation where she had taken time off from her successful business painting murals to have her first child. Now that she needed to support herself as a single mom, she knew it was time to do it full time again. She told me her focus was to double her income in the next 6 months.

Jenny expected me to give her practical marketing tips or guide her to some business resources she could use. I talked with her about going deeper into her own intuition instead. I trusted that she had the answers, yet she didn't. Jenny was resistant to the idea at first. She slowly began to open to the possibility of getting what she needed. I explained the significance of a Reflection Exercise to her, and we proceeded to do one around her goal of doubling her business.

I guide Jenny to tap into her intuition, her inner wisdom, by slowing down, clearing thoughts and using deep breathing to let images or ideas come into her awareness.

I asked her to repeat her goal of doubling her income in her mural business, and see what she needed to do.

Being an artist and very creative, Jenny shared the first thing she saw was an image of doing paintings on canvas in her own studio.

She thought this was the silliest thing she could ever do and that she was obviously getting this whole "Reflection Exercise" thing all wrong. Jenny couldn't imagine why doing paintings for herself was needed to get clients to hire her to paint murals on their walls??

Jenny told me she might have missed something because she thought she had clearly failed at coming up with something useful.

I began talking about the value of honoring our intuition. I helped her see that she did feel clear about getting these images from her inner knowing, and that she didn't just make them up. I challenged Jenny to see that her intuition was talking to her, so why not honor it?

Jenny committed to follow through on the inner wisdom she got from the Reflection Exercise. She decided to make paintings related to what she learned about herself at the retreat. Jenny agreed to set a goal to complete five paintings over the next 4 weeks.

Jenny stuck with it, even though she doubted it would help her on a business level. Painting for herself often felt like a "waste of time", but she did notice an ongoing sense of being on the right track. Something was clicking for her.

Jenny decided to attend a second retreat weekend. Her paintings were done, and she thought it would be fun to bring them along to share with a few of the new friends she had met there. When Jenny arrived at the hotel, her roommate was entertaining a few people in their room for a cocktail gathering. One of the women was attracted to her paintings exclaiming, "I didn't know you were an artist!" She shared about writing a children's book that she is looking for the right illustrator. Jenny's style seemed perfect for what she wanted. They scheduled a meeting to discuss the project, and eventually Jenny signed a contract that literally doubled her business income, *just like she wanted*.

We celebrated her amazing intuition and her even more amazing fearlessness to listen to it. Jenny has a new power of putting the part of herself that "thinks she knows everything" aside.

She says she's thrilled to be leading her business from INTUITION.

"And the best part is the more she tap into it, the stronger it supports her."

ELEMENT #11:
Presence

PERSONAL LEADERSHIP	**BOUNDARIES**	**COMMITMENT**
CHOICE	**PROJECTION**	**INTEGRITY**
SURRENDER	**FORGIVENESS**	**ACCEPTANCE**
INTUITION	**PRESENCE**	**HONORING SELF**

"Let us not pray to be sheltered from dangers but to be fearless when facing them." -Rabindrandath Tagore

Being fully present with another person is a tremendous gift and a powerful way to be in service. Truly BEING with someone requires presence of mind, presence of heart, and physical presence (optional).

Fearless Living is best expressed from a state of presence, in other words, you are fully inhabiting the present moment with all of your being. You are free from distractions, you are not attached to an agenda or an outcome and you have let go of any judgments.

Presence is power. To be present, to be in the moment, that is your only goal.

How does it feel when you are with someone who is truly present? Now consider the opposite expression: How does it feel to interact with someone who is distracted or unable to connect?

If we are attached to a certain outcome, we have already limited our ability to create in the highest way.

Attachments are typically fear-based, from a need to control, which uses a lot of our energy to uphold. Releasing all attachment by choosing to be fully present gives us an abundant resource of energy.

The greatest gift you can give someone is presence. When I lead my interactive workshops, I teach the audience how to be 100% present with each other. The results are beyond description. What I hear from the attendees is that they've never felt so "held," safe, and accepted in their lives.

In order to be completely present with someone else, you must first learn how to be present with yourself. This is about learning to listen to your intuition, being willing to feel all of your emotions, even the ones that you don't care to feel and just allow all of it to come into your awareness.

Once you learn this technique and use it in your relationships, your life will dramatically shift.

Beliefs about Presence

Notice what you believe about presence. Notice your thoughts, attitudes and perceptions about your ability to be present and the level of presence you see in others.

Perhaps you are used to multi-tasking or doing more than one thing at a time. Do you believe this is your most productive option?

Give yourself room to notice the power of presence by first tuning into your beliefs and slowing down enough to choose wisely about how you spend your attention.

EXAMPLES OF BELIEFS ABOUT PRESENCE.

Presence is power.

Presence is essential.

Presence is resourceful.

I am most effective when my focus is spent consciously.

Being mindful about how I spend my attention is my priority.

When I am PRESENT, I offer the gift of being fully with another person.

When we are present we are free from distractions and judgements and it's easy to see our flexibility and capacity to handle whatever happens.

Being present relieves the negative outcomes of attachments, especially when they do not serve us.

Presence Qualities

Imagine your higher self, the fullest expression of your being. When you see this version of yourself, how would you describe the qualities about your presence? Can you imagine the ease and effortless of naturally being fully present to all things?

How would you describe a person who is fully present?

They are open.

They are energized.

Being with them feels grounded.

Their energy is available.

They exhibit a mindfulness and peacefulness.

They have no need to solicit advice or opinion.

They are selfless.

"Daisy and the Deer: A Lesson on Presence."

My best friend ever was my golden retriever, Daisy. She became my guru and I often wondered who was the more spiritually evolved; me or her.

How one sentient being could teach me so much without ever saying a word always intrigued me. Daisy taught me to value presence in my own personal development as well as in all my relationships. I loved how she could sense what was going on in me, whether I was anxious, tired, happy, or annoyed. She taught me the gift of this level of presence.

I was completely drawn in to the way she could be naturally present in every single moment. I came to realize how presence and intuition go hand in hand. Daisy showed me that you can't access your intuition if you are not completely present in the moment. Being present happens naturally when we are intuiting, accessing divine wisdom in any given moment.

I felt completely connected to my dear Daisy. She taught me how to be present just by watching her, ironically by being present in that moment.

I noticed how much more sensitive she was to sounds and smells compared to my senses. I noticed that she was so in the moment, unlike my wandering and fleeting attention span. I noticed how my mind was typically elsewhere, except for when I watched her just be. There was nothing else going on in her head than her experience in the moment. And I could see that by that level of presence, she had an inner knowing and a natural calm.

Daisy, of course being a dog, didn't try to figure anything out, analyze, rationalize, accuse or justify. She only responded to whatever the universe offered her in each moment.

Having her around me all the time, as she loved to follow me around the house and my yard, was like having a "presence teacher" 24/7. I continued to study her behavior because she gave me a sense of calm. She reminded me that there was nothing to worry about and that worrying wouldn't make a difference regardless!

We became meditation buddies as I fed off of her sense of peace and calm. As I did I began to develop my intuition in ways that I never imagined. My senses became more vivid. I was hearing more because I was listening at a deeper level. I was being present. I was seeing more. The sounds of the birds chirping became so much more beautiful. The wind blowing through the leaves of the trees almost sounded like a melody to me. Colors became more vivid.

Not only was I listening at a deeper level externally, I was doing the same internally and it opened up my internal world in a new way. I became so much more in touch with my inner wisdom. I was able to observe my thoughts and the feelings that were reflected in my thoughts.

I had a big "A-ha Moment" when I realized that what prevented me from being as present was my fears.

Fear has our minds dwelling on our past, our mistakes, judgments and regrets, and fear has us anxious by worrying about the future. So of course I was unable to be present! My mind wouldn't allow me. Being fixated on my fearful thoughts blocked my ability to intuit the wisdom that was available in the moment.

So I practiced and I practiced some more. Through Daisy's "teachings" my new level of awareness continued to increase so much that I was accessing my intuition in ways that had me feeling inspired more and more every day.

I realized that I was intuitively communicating with Daisy! It was already happening with the lessons I had gained from her.

One beautiful day in the Fall I had a fabulous experience with the wisdom I was learning from my sweet dog. The majority of the leaves had already fallen from the maple, ash and other various deciduous trees in my back yard. My back yard was heavily wooded and during the spring and summer, my yard was quite private. However, in the fall, as the leaves continued to float down to the ground, the view opened up allowing me to see deeper into the wooded area.

That particular day, much to my surprise, a deer showed up, standing at the edge of my property. I intuited a message, yet I hadn't a clue what it was. It was the first time I had seen a deer in my back yard and I found it a bit odd, but I was still overjoyed that it had paid me a visit.

The deer stared at me with its beautiful eyes and then gracefully walked back into the depth of the woods. I sensed something wasn't right with the deer.

I meditated on the deer sighting, trusting that it showed up to teach me a lesson. Weeks went by and I was still waiting for a message. I sensed that the deer was dead. I felt like I just "knew" it.

I sat down with Daisy and asked her to teach me what I needed to know about the deer sighting. We went into the back yard and she started walking towards the back. I followed her as we went deeper into the woods. I could tell that she wasn't just exploring. She was confidently taking me somewhere. After a few minutes she stopped. I looked down to see the deer carcass! I was stunned! My intuition was right on.

These two animals offered an incredible lesson in presence and intuition. Because of my willingness to let go of my mental chatter, set my fearful thoughts aside and be present to the moment, I learned the power of trusting in the moment and the wisdom that is available!

I realized how much I've denied myself by living in the past or future, by allowing my fear to keep me from being "right here and right now." This was a pivotal moment for me. I am grateful for the lesson, tool and strategy I have been able to use for my ongoing spiritual and emotional development.

Needless to say, when Daisy passed away, I felt a huge loss. Yet the lesson continues because I can still access her level of presence, which is mine as well. I am guided by my inner wisdom now more than ever. This lesson has affected all of my relationships, creating miracles with all the people in my life.

The greatest gift you can give to another is the gift of presence.

In order to do that, you must learn to become present with yourself. Being present with your inner world can be scary because it requires that we feel what is there, whether it be fear, joy, sadness, calm, resentment, frustration, etc. Presence requires that we live in our reality versus chasing thoughts they keep us in fantasy. We wait, we procrastinate, justify and excuse ourselves from what truly is in the moment because we are afraid of reality.

Being fearless will only be accessible with presence. Presence allows you to develop a deeper level of self-trust because you are being driven from within, using your intuition to make the choices that serve your highest good.

Daisy and the deer taught me that my I can access the truth. I can trust my gut feelings, and I can believe in my inner wisdom.

As you learn to develop your awareness through presence, you will notice how much more you see, feel, hear, taste, and smell. Daisy taught me that keen awareness allows me to experience so much more in my relationships.

Fear is not real. Presence is. Which will you choose?

ELEMENT #12:
Honoring Self

PERSONAL LEADERSHIP	BOUNDARIES	COMMITMENT
CHOICE	PROJECTION	INTEGRITY
SURRENDER	FORGIVENESS	ACCEPTANCE
INTUITION	PRESENCE	HONORING SELF

"Being fearless isn't the point. That's impossible. It's learning how to be free from your fear."
-Anonymous

Living fearlessly, we get to walk our talk. When we are modeling our values and what matters most, our impact is greater, our fulfillment is higher and our passion for living fearlessly grows.

In order to truly honor others, we must first learn to honor ourselves. We must accept the mission that allows our own needs to be met so that we can fully support others. This requires a powerful commitment to self-care.

If we are not taking care of ourselves and getting our needs met, it's easy to slip into negative patterns of self-sabotage, co-dependence, and simply being arrogant. We must align our beliefs about the importance of self-care so that our leadership can naturally flourish in ways that ultimately honor ourselves in the long run.

Honoring self is not about self-absorption. Instead, it's about having the awareness to act in a way that will support the greatest expression of yourself in order to serve others and be your best. It's about getting your needs me and practicing self-care daily - "The Me" - in order to best serve "The We."

Beliefs about Honoring Self

Notice your thoughts and attitudes toward self-care.

Perhaps you typically believe that it's selfish to put yourself first. You might believe that taking care of others should always be the first priority, and that you can only put your needs after the needs of others.

Notice if the idea of HONORING YOURSELF conjures negative or uncomfortable feelings. Do you believe at some level it's not okay to honor yourself?

It's time to choose beliefs that expand your ability to honor yourself as a benevolent act of fearlessness.

EXAMPLES OF BELIEFS ABOUT HONORING SELF

My level of self-care inspires everyone around me.

Honoring myself is a reflection of my inner strength.

My self-care is my ongoing project.

Being fearless naturally promotes the loving priority of my self-care.

Honoring myself allows me to model exactly what I want to see in my family.

Honoring Self Qualities

Get in touch with your fully expressed self. Breathe into this part of you fully connected to your inner wisdom and your connection to the divine. When you become present to this expression of yourself, how would you describe your self-care?

How would you describe a person who honors themselves?

They are deserving.

They are worthy.

Their energy is loving and inspiring to others.

They are natural leaders.

They are healthy in body, mind and spirit.

They value self-care.

Journaling Exercise

What would it feel like if you were in a consistent mode of honoring yourself?

What feelings will you have more of by honoring yourself on a daily basis?

What might get in the way of having a practice of honoring yourself? What reason, story or excuse?

A Perspective on Honoring Yourself

Honoring yourself is the recognition that you are worthy of love, acceptance, acknowledgment and good things, just because you are you!

Honoring yourself does not need to depend on any activity, accomplishment or deed.

You are worthy of all the honor, respect and loving attention that you would give to someone you greatly admire....because you are them.

"Pneumonia Became My Hero."

I was 7 years old and in second grade and came down with pneumonia. All I remembered was being admitted to St. James Hospital in Chicago Heights, Illinois.

At that time, the nurses were nuns and they wore habits that scared me. They seemed so rigid, cold and almost robotic. Did they have hair? Why can't they wear make-up? Are they really married to God?

I attended Catholic school when I was growing up, and I remember that some of the nuns were warm and compassionate, but that didn't seem to be the case at the hospital. They seemed mean and angry, at least from what I remember.

For whatever reason, they put 7 year olds in cribs in the early 60's. That in itself made me feel imprisoned. Did they really think I would fall out of bed?

I remember my mom and dad being with me in the hospital, and then my paternal grandparents coming to visit. Grandpa brought me a live plant in a vase in the shape of a puppy. I still have it and cherish it 55 years later.

Evening rolled by and I was told that everybody had to leave; except of course, for me! WHAT? I can't stay here with these scary nuns in this stark old crib all by myself! NO! I began to cry. I began to sob! I was scared. This can't happen to me! The people in my life who make me feel safe and secure are leaving? Please, god, don't let this happen!

And it did happen. I remember watching them leave my room and I was kicking and screaming. I think I recall one of the nuns needing to hold me down. I was never so devastated, feeling so very alone. How could they leave me? How could they make the nurses more important than me? Don't they love me? Will they come back?

When?

To this day, I can still smell the sheets of that crib. I don't know how I was able to sleep that night. I must have cried myself to sleep.

I never realized how traumatic this event was until I started doing some internal work. I was guided into a visualization and this whole scene appeared. I really came to understand how this event shaped my reality.

I was able to identify the beliefs that I've carried around with me ever since I was 7 years old. By what I experienced as abandonment at this young age I decided that I wasn't good enough and that people that love me will leave me. So that meant I really couldn't trust even the ones I love and that I think love me.

Of course my mom and dad came back and took me home. I don't remember anything after that, yet all of the beliefs I created because of that horrific night stayed with me.

I brought those beliefs into my relationships. Because I believed I would be abandoned by those I love, I chose men who would abandon me; emotional abandonment. These choices allowed me to keep proving to myself once again, that I can't trust those I love.

I got to continue to believe that I wasn't good enough to be with someone who I could totally trust. Feeling abandoned became familiar to me and what I knew best. Yet it became toxic and the relationships ended.

My moment of enlightenment was that none of this was true! This was a story that I created because it was what made sense to me. I lived in that story for decades: Until I chose to see something outside of the perspective I chose as a child. I got to see that the only one who can abandon me is me and that's what I was doing.

Choosing to be in relationship with those I really couldn't trust had me abandoning myself. I abandoned myself time after time but not listening to my inner voice. I abandoned myself by trying to trust someone who wasn't trustworthy instead of trusting my gut.

I abandoned myself by repeatedly giving my partner the benefit of the doubt, all the while knowing what was true.

My fear of abandonment is no longer a fear. I now know how to trust and honor myself. And because of that scary hospital stay at 7, I have turned that fearful experience into a gift; a lesson.

Because of it, I realized that I'm the only one who can truly abandon me. I have no control whether or not someone I love exits my life, but I know that I will never abandon myself by continuing to honor myself, being present with myself and intuiting what is for the highest good.

Honoring self, ultimately is about applying all of the 12 Elements of Fearless Living. Of course, I wish I could go back in time and re-do so many aspects of my past by applying Fearless Living, however, I have immense gratitude for each and every moment.

Pneumonia brought me to right here and right now; a place of self-honor. And the greatest reward that I've experience by honoring myself, is the passion that has been cultivated to be a contribution and support others to do exactly the same!

Reflection Exercise for Honoring Yourself

Use this exercise to practice self-care.

We go inside for internal wisdom. Take yourself into a quiet zone. Sit comfortably and begin meditating or just focusing on breathing. Noticing our internal flame is a powerful way to boost energy while eliminating those feelings that diminish our flame.

This exercise is easy to use wherever you are.

Visualize Your Inner Flame:

Imagine a fire in your fireplace.

> *Surrounded by oxygen, the fire burns brightly. Without oxygen, there can be no flame.*

> *Each of us have our own internal flame inside. Just like the fire in your fireplace, our internal flame needs air.*

> *If you stop breathing, the fire inside of you will be diminished.*

Use your breath to feed your flame.

> *Our internal flame gives us calm, joy, ease, peacefulness.*

> *When you feel negative energy (anxious, sad, pressured and alone,) your body contracts. When your body tightens up, your internal flame is not getting enough oxygen.*

When you start to feel anxious, take some deep breaths.

Imagine with each breath, you are igniting your internal flame.

Take as many deep breaths as you need, until you feel your body start to soften.

Notice the tight feelings in your body starting to loosen up.

Continue breathing and visualizing your internal flame burning brightly and giving you all the energy you need.

Last, ask yourself:

"What's one action I can take today to honor myself?"

Practice this exercise daily.

As often as you can, take a moment to consider how brightly your internal flame is burning.

Send some breath to your internal flame and notice that you can control your feelings, live fearlessly, and achieve your goals doing it!

Integrating the Twelve Elements

Tell me, what is it you plan to do with your one wild and precious life?
-Mary Oliver

Now that you have experienced this book, I invite you to step fully into your fearless self.

You are now able to see the distinctions between playing small (FEAR) and playing full-out (FEARLESS), and I invite you to celebrate this powerful awareness.

You now have the ability to choose beliefs that support your fearless self.

You now have an unstoppable understanding of the qualities that define your fearless self.

Compare your awareness to what you remember at the moment you began the book, and make an assessment of your evolution.

Perhaps you notice multiple breakthroughs and changes. Perhaps you notice one or two shifts in perspective. There is no hierarchy to elements of transformation.

Fearless Living in Action

Take your first step as a FEARLESS LIVING LEADER and acknowledge yourself for three things you experienced in this book.

1._____

_____

2._____

_____

3._____

_____

"I Am Fearless"

(Your signature here.)

A Poem about Fearless Living

New vistas appearing
-- new possibilities –
always, growing to fruition:
This is my new life.

"I Am Fearless"
this way to be living,
stepping, or leaping again
off a cliff, or airplane,
where the net always appears
once I choose to act.

It has changed me.
Now I am big enough
to include the world.

There is compassion, or knowledge,
or a smile, and more, for everyone.

-Written by a student in the Fearless Living Leadership Training

About Debbie Leoni

Teaching personal development and positive change through body, mind and spirit has been the strong foundation for much of Debbie Leoni's career over the past twenty-plus years.

Drawing on her background in the healing arts teaching yoga, meditation, and leading spiritual retreats, Debbie provides transformational value through her powerful focus, intuition and personal brand of inspired leadership.

As a Fearless Living coach, workshop leader, and international speaker, Debbie truly understands how the path from fear into courage compliments personal development in all areas of life.

Her intention is to create the inspiration and the structure for fearless living that is simple enough, challenging enough and delivers lasting results.

Debbie blends a wealth of wisdom and life-experience with her passion for transformation to create a unique approach to her work. Whether she is leading Fearless Living Workshops, teaching Leadership Training Programs, or coaching individuals or groups in Fearless Living Programs, she supports people through their own journey from fear into courage, leading them into a fuller expression of the life they desire.

Debbie has two sons, four grandchildren and lives outside of Chicago, IL.

A Personal Note from Debbie:

I am in love with understanding the human spirit through the perspective of thoughts, energy, emotions and the body.

Throughout my career path as a Yoga Teacher, Fitness Trainer, Weight Management Coach, Reiki Practitioner, Spiritual Director and Certified Life Coach, I am passionate about integrating my skills and wisdom into helping others lead fulfilling lives.

I am committed to "walk the talk" of Fearless Living by speaking, coaching, writing and leading transformative events. I am delighted to share this journey with you here.

~ Debbie Leoni

Visit my website for more information:

www.debbieleoni.com

Need a Speaker?

Do you know of an organization that would benefit from a presentation based on topics from *"The Twelve Elements of Fearless Living?"*

Debbie Leoni travels from Chicago, Illinois and welcomes opportunities to speak to groups, and at events and conferences.

With over 1500 hours of training from a variety of sources, a list of relevant certifications, and over 20 years of experience as a professional coach and facilitator, Debbie is well respected in the industry. She is also internationally recognized as a speaker, group facilitator and retreat leader.

Please email us to inquire: iamfearless@debbieleoni.com

Opportunities to Connect:

"If your actions inspire others to dream more, learn more, do more and become more, you are a leader."
—John Quincy Adams

Mention this book to receive a complimentary **"Fearless Living Strategy"** a 20-minute coaching session with Debbie Leoni.

Subscribe to our newsletter to receive a copy of Debbie's **Guided Meditation recording, "From Fear to Calm."**

Connect with Debbie on Facebook and join the conversation: www. facebook.com/dleoni

Contact us for speaking events, workshops or presentations:

iamfearless@debbieleoni.com

Acknowledgements

Thank you to my entire family – I love you more than life itself. Because of you, I know what matters most.

Thank you to all of those who have taken this work and created a ripple effect. You are making my purpose real by helping to change the world with fearlessness.

Thank you to my beloved teacher and mentor, the late Debbie Ford. Your example and courage inspired my passion for fearlessness in countless ways.

Thank you to the late Rev. Donald Castle, the most powerful spiritual teacher of my life. He taught me to be a selfless servant. He was the purest example of Christ-Consciousness, teaching me compassion, acceptance, and unconditional love for everyone.

I am especially grateful for the partnership I have created with the talented and fearless Jenifer Novak Landers, author of "Fully Expressed Living". This book would not be possible without her creativity, support, writing contributions and her ability to reflect and share my vision of Fearless Living.

Thank you to Karl Palachuk, of Great Little Book Publishing for his expert guidance in getting this book published.

CPSIA information can be obtained
at www.ICGtesting.com
Printed in the USA
FSOW01n0958050516
20088FS